PRICING STRATEGIES: MAKING THE MOST FROM YOUR HARD WORK

BOOK 5 OF THE SUCCESSFUL INDIE AUTHOR SERIES

CRAIG MARTELLE

Editing services provided by Joe Martin
Cover by Sapphire Designs
Formatting (both eBook and paperback) by Drew Avera

This is a book on writing books. If that wasn't your desire in buying this eBook, then please return it within seven days for a full refund from Amazon.

TABLE OF CONTENTS

Chapter 3: What are those prices...37

Chapter 4: Managing Reader Expectations...66

INTRODUCTION

What is the best price where you make the most money? Higher isn't necessarily better. Lower isn't necessarily more attractive. You have to find the best fit for your brand to draw the most readers willing to pay that right price.

What is the psychology of pricing? How do readers react to a book that's free or maybe 99 cents? Why do we always price at $xx.99—can't we make it an ever four bucks?

Not if you want to sell more books. One percent here, five percent there, and all of a sudden, the sales number becomes significant. The greater the sales, the greater that one percent becomes.

That's what this book is about—decrypting book pricing in an easy-to-digest way with just a taste-tempter of data geekery for those so inclined (if you want the full exploration of the numbers behind the scene, this book isn't for you—I started to do that but the time investment was more than I was willing to pay). You can skip the math problems, although the ones I include are important.

I'll put the bottom line up front. This book is called

Pricing Strategies because there are strategies that you should adopt, embrace, and stay with to be least confusing to your established readership and any new readers you might bring on board as you identify your brand and slap a price on it.

Do you want more readers? Then maybe you pimp that first book far and wide, spending tens of thousands of dollars on ad campaigns and promotions because you know it's a great book and once people read it, they'll be moving to the rest of the books in your series. And that's where you make your money. Milk is cheap in the United States, and it runs out with great and untimely frequency. Grocery stores put it as far from the front door as possible, so you have to walk through the entire store to get it. They do that on purpose. Giving away a book for free to get an email address is a little bit of the same. It's called marketing. You get something, but I'm going to show you all these other taste-tempting somethings along the way.

What does your author brand tell readers? The price of your books plays a role in that. Regular prices, discount prices, promotions, omnibuses, and so many other ways to price yourself into or out of existence. Are you playing the long game? If you just want to sell one book, this book isn't for you. This book is for professional authors who want to make a career of writing, even if you don't do it full time. You can still make full-time money with a great book and then more great books.

There will be plenty of if-then statements, because you'll have triggers in pricing that tell you whether you're too low or too high. Unfortunately, your sale and promotions may have already run their course, but the best news is that there *will* be a next time. Study your numbers and improve your strategy to make more with your next promotion. There's enough turnover on lists that you can hit the same promotions once every six to twelve months with little degradation in return.

Make the most you can. Why price a book at $0.99 if the same number of people will buy it at $2.99? Why price a book at $2.99 if no one will buy it at that price? Maybe there's a reason. And for the pricing strategies I discuss here, I'm assuming you have a decent book, a genre-appropriate cover, and your blurb is good.

I don't share a great deal of my numbers in this book because those would have made the book unwieldy, but I've included enough to reinforce my main points. I have a few sexy graphs and such, most from BookReport (an add-on that puts your Amazon KDP data into a more useful format). I sell from 3,000 to 10,000 books a month. That may sound like a lot, but it could be more and how can I make sure that I get every bit of profit from each of my more than 100 titles, all while keeping my readers happy?

How do you balance those seemingly competing interests?

Managing your reader expectations while running marketing campaigns to bring in more readers. Pricing brings home the money. If people gave their books away, they wouldn't be feeding themselves or their families. You can give all your stuff away in a hundred and fifty years when your books are in the public domain.

Until then, let's make a little something for us.

CHAPTER ONE

Setting Yourself Up for Success

- What is the potential?
- Terms and Definitions
- Linear calculations
- Regular Price
- Advertising
- Marketing

Self-flagellation is no way to go through life. Learn what you need to know without donating your hard earnings by having misaligned prices. Don't beat yourself with pennies when dollar bills are to be had.

What is the potential?

I wish I knew what I had in mind when I put this section header into my outline. Maybe I wanted to talk about 70%

royalty versus 35%. Maybe I wanted to talk about ten readers coming on board because of a discount instead of just one buying your book at full price. Maybe I wanted to talk about the absolute highest price you could charge and still find readers willing to pay it.

There is so much potential to make money and an infinite number of ways to do it, most of which fall under three approaches.

1. Sell a lot of something, making a little bit from each sale (the Walmart model)
2. Sell few of something but make a lot from each sale (the Ferrari model)
3. Get people into your store and then they buy things (Godiva chocolate factory tour)

I see everything as a subset of those simple premises. The model names are mine. I'm sure there's an MBA term for this stuff, but I don't care about those. I care about making this easy to understand because pricing models can be complex. Geeky and complex are fine for some people, but then there are the rest of us. I use spreadsheets for calculations to give me exact numbers, and then I back out to the macro view and use that to drive how I price my books in order to make as much as possible from each sale while still garnering more sales.

I may sell an overpriced book once, but if that makes the reader shy away or if I get them to buy at full price, then they come across a sale ad, they are going to feel slighted. Even if they like the book, they might not come back. No one wants to support someone who comes across as shady.

So don't do shady things. I put dates on my social media posts to be extra clear: Free! Today (October 8, 2019) Only...

No surprises, unless it's pleasantly surprised, like the readers who love your stories, those people who haven't read any book in years, but something about your blurb drew them in. They bought it on sale, but now they can't wait for the next book and are more than happy to pay full price to get it on release day. Those readers are worth their weight in gold. Treat them as such.

The broad reach of a 99-cent sale or the siren's call of FREE! have their places. One pays for itself quicker than the other.

You'll get more downloads of books that are discounted to zero than you will of books that are a dollar. But how many of those who downloaded it for free are going to read it? I prefer putting a book on sale for $0.99 because the potential reader has some buy-in for the book, making them more likely to read it. I write series and have a lot of books, so getting someone into one of my books can lead them to the rest. That could mean hundreds of dollars in revenue from a single superfan.

The potential of making or losing a great deal of money is there. You'll need to do some other things that we'll talk about. You need to have a great cover that is appropriate for your genre, a blurb that compels readers to buy, and then a price point that doesn't turn the readers off. You want them to one-click your book.

You reap the rewards. Now repeat that with ten thousand readers and you're going to have a great week.

I'm going to talk about the perception of value. How do readers respond when they see books that don't cost what they expect? All this and more. Pricing Strategies. Let's establish some common terminology before we move on.

. . .

Author's determination of value based on work put into a book

Here's a simple formula I came up with to help you calculate this.

$$\frac{\text{Author Time \& Money Investment}}{\text{Author Time \& Money Investment}} - 1 + \text{What the Market will Bear} = \text{Price of Your Book}$$

The math comes out to one minus one plus what the market will bear. The only thing that matters is what the market will bear. Unless you have a professional marketing research team, you have to figure out what the market will bear all by yourself, but it isn't daunting. It's what this book is about.

This isn't to denigrate your time or effort in writing your book. But—and it's a huge but—you need to put on your business hat when you sell your art. I want you to get the most from your book, and that means trying some things that have worked and shaping your expectations appropriately. Your forty-page ebook could be worth $1,000 of your life, and you can put that price on it if you want, but don't be surprised if you don't sell any copies.

Terms and Definitions

Let's talk about some words where we need shared definitions.

General Terms

Books—I use the term "books" as a synonym for stories.

"Book" has no defined length. Novel, on the other hand, is defined by the Romance Writers of America (RWA) and the Science Fiction and Fantasy Writers of America (SFWA) because of the awards both organizations sponsor. According to their guidelines, here are those specific terms.

Novel = 40,000 words or longer

Novella =17,500 words up to 40,000 words

Novelette = 7,500 words up to 17,500 words

Short story = 2,500 words up to 7,500 words

Flash fiction = under 2,500 words

Box Set & Omnibus—technically, a box set is a collection of physical books contained within a physical box while an omnibus is a collection of full-length books under a single cover. With the advent of ebooks, these definitions have blurred and are used synonymously, except occasionally, Amazon has taken exception and prefers you use omnibus for a digital collection of full-length books. I use omnibus with Amazon and box set for casual conversation. An anthology is a collection of shorter works under a single cover. Anthologies are usually works from different authors. I've used it for my short story collections. Others will use the term "collection" for bundles of shorter works by one author.

KDP Select (also called Kindle Unlimited)—This is for ebooks exclusively with Amazon and which participate in the subscription reading program. The ebooks cannot be available digitally anywhere else. In return, your exclusive books earn page reads from the Kindle Unlimited program. It has some benefits and some limitations. I make a lot more money being exclusive than I do wide, so most of my books are available through the Kindle Unlimited (KU) subscription service. Here's a tip—you don't have to be exclusive to Amazon to select the 70% royalty rate. The difference between 70%

and 35% (besides the math) is that you will get charged a download fee based on the size of your ebook file at the 70% rate. In some markets, you must be in Select to get the 70% royalty rate, India, for example, where other markets won't pay 70% regardless. These sales are from countries that don't have their own Amazon store and their buyers use the Amazon.com store. There is no download fee at the 35% rate.

Read-through is specific to Amazon's KU program. It is where a reader will check out the next book in your series. I use it interchangeably with buy-through. When an author is exclusive to Amazon, they can put their book in KU, where authors get paid by the number of pages Amazon's KU reading subscribers read. The pricing is usually between $0.004 and $0.005 per page read. A book priced at $2.99 and 70% royalties will earn roughly $2.00 (that takes into account the download cost as well—you don't really get a full 70%, but this is far better than traditional publishing contracts). To earn $2.00 through page reads, your book needs to be between four hundred and five hundred pages. I think it's clear that if your book is that long, you won't have it priced at $2.99. But KU readers aren't the same as buyers. These are separate population, so it's better getting $1 on a sale than no sale, while others draw $2. That is my business premise. There are wildly successful authors who don't participate in KU, where all their income is through sales. That simply requires a different marketing approach. I have books that are exclusive, and I have books that are not. But read-through is critical. You need the readers to read through to the next book in the series. This is most obvious when they do not and your page reads for a book hover around zero.

Buy-through—this is when buyers go on to buy book two after picking up book one (or later books in a series). A good buy-through rate from one to two is 50%, unless you had book one for free, then it's closer to two to ten percent. Book two to three should be higher. I always look for at least 80%. If I don't get that, there might be something wrong with book two. Generally, if I can get someone to book three in one of my series, my read-through rate goes north of 90%. The readers are always the final arbiter of whether a book is good or not. If they aren't buying it and they were former fans, it's either that they don't know about it or they got turned off during the last book.

Release, launch, and publish—I use these as synonyms. They all mean the same thing—getting that book to market.

Wide—any author who is not exclusive (digital books/ebooks only) to Amazon. Wide means the book can be published to Apple books, Kobo, Barnes & Noble, BookFunnel, Smashwords, libraries, or any other place that carries digital content.

Back matter—everything in your book after The End (or whatever term you use to finish the current book). The back matter will contain your calls to action—join your newsletter, visit your website, look at your other books, learn a bit about you in your *Author Note*.

Front matter—the stuff up front in your book. A copyright page, a table of contents (I don't put them in my fiction books, but Amazon's automation process adds it), maybe a dedication, maybe some terms used in the book, possibly a call to action—newsletter and social media. I put both front and back matter in my books. I don't think I can remind my readers often enough that they can find me on the internet (my clearly-named website—craigmartelle.com, Facebook, and BookBub).

Categories & genres—I use these interchangeably since they are constructs within the publishing industry. On Amazon, a category depicts a genre or sub-genre. Also, genre = marketing. I define genre as the biggest group of readers who will like your book.

Marketing Terms

Tail—this is a term that relates to book sales after a launch or promotion. Each publication almost always has a spike, those high sales within the first few days of release or a major promotion where the most people buy, but after that, as sales drop, that is the tail. We want the biggest tail for the longest amount of time. A month of additional sales is a great tail. Some have a week or two. Some have three months. The longer the tail, the more ancillary factors are working in your favor (like word of mouth, read-through, snowballing, going viral on social media, and so on). These are sales without additional spend.

Promotion—this is where you conduct a very specific campaign (getting a BookBub Featured Deal, for example, is a promotion), maybe surge a few newsletter swaps over a short period where you have your book at $0.99 or even free. I am presently trying to run two promotions a month from my different series. One book. One promotion. Then look for the read-through/buy-through.

Ads—advertising—a promotion is a type of advertising, but when I talk ads, these are for your books, usually at full price, and they are ongoing campaigns where you run your ad for weeks or months at a time before changing up graphics or ad text or targeted audience. Amazon advertising, Facebook ads, Kobo ads (if wide), Google AdWords, and BookBub ads (not to be confused with a featured deal) are the primary advertising platforms. I also run ads on books that are on sale (as a separate track to get readers into my books just in case a promotion hasn't reached them). Promotions and new releases are usually your big sales bumps, but your daily bread and butter will be ads. When I talk about ad spend, this is it. Keep your books in front of readers at all times, as often as reasonable.

Stacking ads—The practice of using multiple paid promotions to reinforce and support the process of maximizing sales of your book during a fixed period of time. It's the effort to put your book before as many readers as possible across a variety of platforms.

Sale—This is when you drop the price of your book for a limited period. It is part of your marketing strategy and generally used in conjunction with a promotion.

A/B Testing—Amazon Advertising as well as Facebook ads have this option. A/B testing (also known as split testing or bucket testing) is a method of comparing two versions of an ad against each other to determine which one performs better. Then you use the better-performing one as you scale up your ad campaign.

Financial Terms

Margin (profit margin)—how much you make from a sale (and overall). A book also has a physical margin, the space between the text and the outside of the page. But in this book, when I say "margin," I'm talking about money. The formula is: (net sales minus cost of goods sold)/net sales. Simple as that. Is it greater than zero or less than zero? And you can't divide by zero if that's the case. Net sales are the total revenue you earn from a book (he royalty minus any distributor costs like Amazon's download fee). If you sell one book and the distributor pays you $3.47, that is your net. Cost of goods sold includes everything you've paid: cost of your cover, your editing, your marketing, all your costs. If you have few sales, then you need to reduce your cost of goods sold, from a business perspective, unless you have a hard minimum on your costs. If you spend $1500 on producing a book, you need to make more than $1500 in sales, but margin as it applies to single books is misleading. A first book could be a loss-leader, you give it away to generate interest in your series which gives you a negative margin. You're not going to cancel your first books because they're not profitable. That's why it's most important to look at margin from a macro level – all of your revenue minus all of your costs. That's where you want to be in positive territory. Read on.

$$\frac{\text{Net Sales} - \text{Cost of Goods Sold}}{\text{Cost of Goods Sold}} = \text{Margin}$$

Royalty rate—the percentage of the book's sale price that goes to the publisher (you, as opposed to the distributor like Amazon, Kobo, or Apple). You need to know what rate you are getting so you can best calculate what you're making per sale.

Earn out—this is when a sale pays the costs to run the ads or the promotions. If you spent $350 on promotions and advertising on a $0.99 book, then you need to sell roughly 1,000 copies to break even (that is, earn out). We always look at how we can improve on that. Having books in a series is especially handy in improving your profitability.

ROI (return on investment)—how much did you earn (net earnings) divided by how much you spent. You have ROI from an ad campaign and you have a more inclusive ROI (an entire series, for example). If you spent a dollar and earned two dollars, you would have a 100% ROI. Here's how the calculation works. Net earnings minus the cost of investment divided by the cost of investment. Or (Net earnings—Ad cost)/Ad cost. This also applies to a book's total cost; if you spent more than you earned from the book, despite successful ads, then you have a negative ROI. I use the terms "revenue" and net earnings interchangeably here, in this case to mean what you, the author/publisher are paid by the distributor (Amazon, for example).

$$\frac{\text{Revenue} - \text{Cost of Investment}}{\text{Cost of Investment}} = \text{ROI}$$

(2-1)/1 or 1/1 = 1 (in percent that's 100%). You'll also hear that result referred to as a 2 to 1 ROI, which means that for every dollar spent, you're getting two dollars back. None of this is intuitive, but that's how the calculations work.

Download fee—If you select the 70% option on Amazon, you'll get charged the download fee. For one of my box sets, the download fee was 49 cents because I included the cover images. It was nearly 3,000 pages, so when I removed the images, it was still 35 cents, but that's fourteen extra cents in my pocket for every sale.

Linear Calculations

Don't be doing no linear calculations! Linear equations

solve for y with a single variable x. They result in a straight line on the Euclidean plane. There are no straight-line earnings in the author business. There are ups and downs and that's why we constantly tinker with pricing, advertising, and promotions.

I use the term linear calculations similarly. This is the tendency to calculate using straight multiples and not using variables or a logarithmic curve. If you made ten dollars today, that doesn't mean you're going to make $10 every day for 365 days and at the end of the year, you will have $3650. This is a linear calculation, and you will suffer mightily if you try to live your author life this way.

A minor miscue that some people believe is that if we have an ROI of 100%, and if we double our spend, we'll double our revenue.

This is where the curveballs come at you. Doubling your spend may only result in increasing your earnings by 50% or maybe even less. You may double your ad spend and not earn anything extra. Incremental scaling up is a completely different challenge and not the subject of this book. I don't know of any book that properly addresses it. I can't write that book, either, as my scaling up efforts have only been partially successful.

I am going to explore calculations in this book, and I'll do my best to make them easy to understand. I'll add a blown-up graphic of the math as well. I'll put the bottom line up front, and then you can embrace, move on, or study more in depth. I want to provide you with as much or as little information as you want.

How about this little tidbit from Joe Solari? In looking at sales curves across multiple genres, all top authors, over an eighteen-month timeframe from launch, eight out of ten times

50% of the revenue is earned in the first six months. Testing is good, but you want to get your prices right sooner than later.

Two times two doesn't necessarily equal four. Welcome to Pricing Strategies.

Regular Price

This is the absolute sweet spot. Regular price is earnings nirvana. Readers buying your book at regular price delivers unto you heavenly bliss. It is what you are working for.

If you can only sell books when you discount them, you need new readers or new books or a different regular price, but something must change. To get a BookBub featured deal, you need to discount your book 50% or more off the regular price. This is a good benchmark for what a regular price should be. Also, Amazon's 70% royalty rate minimum threshold is $2.99 with a maximum of $9.99. Those are the parameters within most regular prices can be found.

It is also your benchmark against which you will measure your own efforts.

Advertising

You advertise anytime you ask someone to buy your stuff. You advertise all the time to get people into your books. You may ratchet up your advertising during a promotion. Advertising is not a dirty word. It's going to make up a large part of your expenses. It will be critical to sustained revenue.

You're going to spend a lot on it, so don't goof it up too much. You have to continuously test. That means you will spend money for no gain despite knowing you don't want to do that exact same thing again.

When you find traction and can expand on it, the money spigots get turned on.

And revenue streams carry their joy in gold-plated gondolas directly to your bank account. Or something like that. And then the ad goes stale and you need to come up with a better one or run a new promotion or adjust your targeting or do a thousand other things.

You cannot rest on your laurels, so stop staring at those golden gondolas. They are metaphorical and can disappear in a heartbeat. Keep advertising smartly, using data and adjusting as you go to stay at the front of your campaigns.

Marketing

An active and robust marketing campaign evens out those peaks and valleys that are part of every earning graph. Marketing is your strategy in which your ads play a key role, as do your promotions, sales, personal appearances, social media presence, newsletters, and more. Marketing is your presence in the world of those who sell stuff.

You just happen to be selling your books, which are made up of your time in turning those ideas into a story or nonfiction title. You have created something from nothing because you have a brain and a way to document those thoughts. It is the best of things to create. Look around you, something created every single thing you see, both inside your home and outside. The beauty, the functionality, the artwork—all of it serves a purpose. That is what you've done, nothing less. Hopefully, others will think of your book as something that serves a purpose in their lives.

Yet, they won't know it exists unless you have a marketing campaign to get it in front of them. This is your strategic planning, starting with genre (remember genre = marketing, don't convolute it any further) so you can plan how to access those readers. You might run promotions, sales, or just hit the ads hard for your book at a regular price. It's important to know what a reader will pay for a book in a certain genre. All of this is marketing.

You need to have an idea of what you want to do above and beyond the generic "sell more books." Here's what a strategic pricing plan looks like for a full-length (70k words) science fiction novel:

1. **Pre-Order period**—Full price of $4.99 (pre-order is to guarantee it launches on the date I want it to).

2. **Launch week**—keep it at full price, begin ads, both auto targeted and manual targeted for specific keywords and similar books, hit Newsletter.

3. **Seven days after launch**—drop price to $0.99 for one day (call it "fan pricing"), send to Newsletter again.

4. **Raise price to full**, review Amazon Advertising campaigns, resend to Newsletter non-opens (the full-price announcement).

5. **Run full-price ad campaign on Facebook.**

6. **Stay engaged** on Facebook. Solicit fans for quotes and reviews.

7. **Go live**—talk about the book two weeks after publication, thank fans who have read and double thanks those who also reviewed.

8. **Launch plus three months**—drop to $0.99 for three days, run paid promotions like Book Barbarian.

9. **One year series discount**—hopefully there
are a bunch of books in the series by this time,
publish first box set.

And so on. That's what a marketing plan looks like. You
can get more detailed with exactly how you're going to target
certain genres. That's good, because you can then see what
resonates and what you can leverage more of.

CHAPTER TWO

Prices and Their Place in the Natural Order

- Free
- $0.99
- $1.99
- $2.99
- $3.99—$4.99
- $5.99—$6.99
- $7.99—$9.99
- Higher

I'm going to use a baseline of US prices, but we'll talk international currencies later. What does the price say about your book? How can that entice a reader? And when does a potential buyer see the price?

If a reader is cost-sensitive, they'll look for the book's price sooner rather than later, but people do a lot of window shopping before buying. Here's a secret that you shouldn't tell anyone. If you price your books for the price-sensitive, you will build a readership that wants you to write for pennies. You'll also not gain readers because they'll think your product is cheap. There are times for sales and there are other times where you should set the hook by making a book available at a discount, but that's part of the marketing process—70% off!

If you want to be able to pay your mortgage with your writing income, you can't be making pennies on the dollar.

Regular price points vary according to author, genre, length, and platform. A 60,000 word novel can be priced anywhere from Free to $14.99, depending on the particulars. BUT—big but here—a $14.99 book can only be sold on Amazon at the 35% royalty rate, which earns an author $5.24, but a $9.99 book at 70% with a $0.10 download fee earns you $6.89. Earn more from a lower price? That seems to be an easy business decision.

As a new author? You probably won't command the higher price, but you can eventually get there on your own if your wide sales are great enough to offset the difference in earnings from Amazon. Never sell yourself short. I started pricing my full-length novels at $2.99 to gain traction. Now, I price everything at $4.99 and get it. Dress for the job you want.

Free

This is a challenging price point because your entire profitability depends on what the potential reader does after he/she downloads your book. Every other price point earns you something with the download because it's a purchased download.

If you make your book free because it's a reader magnet, then they are giving you their email address to get your title. If you are making it free because it's the first in a series, then your bet is that enough of those who downloaded it for free read it and like it enough to buy the second book in the series (and then keep reading and buying).

If you have only one book and you are not using it as a reader magnet, there is no reason to give your book away for free. The downloaders (we won't call them readers, not yet anyway) have nothing else to go to. They will forget you exist before your next book comes out, even if they do read your first. Don't count on them following you on the distributor's page because you have no way to tell for certain that they followed you. Save FREE for when you can monetize the download.

There are also the logistical challenges with setting a book to free. If you're in KDP Select (KU), then you get five free days a quarter per book. That's easy. You schedule them using your KDP bookshelf. They happen exactly when they are supposed to happen. If you are wide, then you have to get Amazon to match the other vendors. Amazon does not automatically do this. They recently changed their terms of service allowing them the flexibility regarding mandatory price matching. How do you get your wide book priced to Free on Amazon? You make it Free on the other platforms and then start emailing and calling Amazon customer service until you get someone who will drop your price to zero.

If you are using an aggregator like Draft2Digital or PublishDrive, then you go through them to get the price set at zero. This isn't something you can make happen easily. Vendors want you to sell more of your products at higher prices because their livelihood is also dependent upon the amount of money that flows through their store.

I have published a number of books wide for various reasons. I have never tried making one free. I usually discount to $0.99 for a promotion like a BookBub Featured Deal (BookBub is a professional newsletter service that has hundreds of thousands of readers on their lists and one typically gets tens of thousands of downloads from a book listed as Free, but they are extremely hard to get and very expensive once you win a spot in their newsletter). If your book is permanently free, you can't get a BookBub Feature because you must discount it at least fifty percent to qualify.

Free is a valid price point and permafree has its place. I have some books for free, but I have them on BookFunnel where people pay me with their email address. It gets them into the other books in my series. It's worth the cost of no revenue for the opportunity to bring them on board. I have over one hundred books, so putting one or five for free is no big deal. It doesn't break the bank.

But what if you only have two books? I wouldn't consider it until I had three, then put the first one for free and promote the hell out of that first book to bring people on board. If your first book reads well, it doesn't take much time before readers start picking up your second and third book. Whale readers, those who consume great quantities of books, will probably wait until three books are published in a series before picking up the first one.

Free is also the price point with the lowest read-through/buy-through rate. Ten percent used to be considered decent, which means that you give ten copies away in the hopes that one person will go to book two (where they pay for your book two, and this is how you make money from a free book). Recent numbers have dropped rather significantly (I think the quality of my books has improved, so it's not because they are lesser). Two to maybe five percent is more in line with what I'm seeing, and it's closer to the two than the five. You need to keep track of these numbers if you want to measure whether giving your book away was worthwhile. If you measure it, you can manage it.

· · ·

$0.99 (ninety-nine cents)—Royalty $0.35

This is the lowest sale price you can offer with Amazon without going through the rigamarole of getting your non-exclusive Amazon title price-matched when it is free elsewhere. Amazon has formally stated that they are not obligated to match the price of other retailers. $0.99 also limits you to a 35% rate on Amazon (but no download fee), unless you do a Countdown Deal (CD) as part of KDP Select where you'll then earn 70% royalty for the US and UK markets only. If you have a BookBub Featured deal with international customers, you cannot split the rates. You have to select the 35% rate and manually change the price to $0.99 for the markets that will be served as part of the deal (US, UK, Can, Aus, and India).

You can have a book permanently priced at $0.99—I do. I don't have it in Kindle Unlimited so I can hawk the book on BookFunnel for free to build a Newsletter List.

$0.99 is the most common price to which authors discount their books for promotions and various visibility-enhancing efforts. Less than a buck is a compelling point. It vastly increases the chance that the buyer will read the book. Even at the almost free price of $0.99, your baseline for read-through/buy-through shoots up to 50%.

During a promotion where I discount a book to $0.99, I'll move far fewer copies than those where the book is Free. Using the same targeting and promotion outlets, I can sell 250-500 books at $0.99 but pricing a book at Free, give away ten times that number. With a two percent read through versus 50%, you can see that I make orders of magnitude more money with a $0.99 discount.

Since the costs for promotion are the same, we won't include those in our calculations.

5,000 books given away for free = $0.00

Two percent buy-through to Book 2 (at $4.99 with a $0.15 download fee yields $3.34 in revenue per copy) means a hundred books to earn $334. Further ROI is strengthened when 90% go on to Book 3 and later in the series.

500 books at $0.99 = $175

50% buy-through to Book 2 ($3.34 in revenue per copy) means 250 books to earn $835. Even if the buy-through to Book 2 is only 25%, that's still $417.50 in revenue plus the initial $175 bringing the initial revenue to $592.50. Your ROI depends on the costs of your promotions, but the chances for a higher ROI is with your $0.99 books. Once you have the readers into Book 3, you've usually hooked them for the whole series. These are the good readers and fans who help you have a career as an author.

That said, I will still run a promotion for a FREE book. Once I've targeted the audiences and brought new readers on board with $0.99, I'll try that same targeting with a FREE book, just to pick up any stragglers who don't want to try a new author, even for a price of less than a dollar. They are out there. I want all the readers, so I don't always do the same thing to vacuum them up.

What about the other platforms? Going through Draft2Digital, my royalties are 60% actual (that's 70% minus the 10% fee, which is 15%, but off the retail price and not 15% off the royalty rate, so it works out to 10%) for Kobo, Barnes & Noble (B&N), and Apple Books. Less expensive books earn more through Draft2Digital, and they earn this same rate, no matter the price. Higher priced individual books get 70% through direct sales on Kobo, B&N, and Apple.

$1.99—Royalty $0.70

This price point appears to be the new $0.99, based on

what I'm seeing from BookBub Featured Deals and promoted through several other paid newsletters. It's like getting a 70% Countdown Deal, because you'll get royalties of $0.70 per copy, but there's the minor drawback—it's twice what most other sales are going for. Enough people might balk at this price for a first in series from a new author. With my backlist, I don't need that many people to come aboard to have a wildly positive ROI, but I prefer bringing as many aboard as possible. I don't see using this price point for discounted first in series for quite some time. I don't think the broader market is quite ready for it.

That said, my Free Trader complete omnibus (nine books, the complete series in one pack of nearly 3,000 pages) is a massive beast, and the minimum price I could drop it to was $1.99. I had already set up a few promotions, but people quickly flexed and I kept all my promotions at the $1.99 price point. I saw no appreciable drop in sales. Better than that, when I saw how many new readers were coming on board because of the sheer volume of a complete set, I saw no difference in sales when I raised the price to $2.99. My royalties at $1.99 were $0.70, but at $2.99 were $1.75 ($0.35 download fee with the 70% royalty rate).

I watch how legacy publishing (traditional publishers, the "Big Five," as it may be) markets their stuff. They are taking a number of spots each month on major promotion sites (like BookBub). They are pricing more and more of their stuff at $1.99 and $2.99. There's still some competition for the $0.99, but if legacy is doing it, is that the trigger that indies are looking for in order to raise our prices?

Not necessarily. Their books still have name recognition. I paid $1.99 this morning for a Clifford D. Simak book that I didn't have. What would compel me to pick up something for $1.99 from an author I don't recognize? A compelling cover and blurb! Those things that make the book look like what I read. I'm not in the minority since I read a lot of mainstream genres where multiple million-selling authors hang out.

$1.99. Get it if you can, though $2.99 is sweeter, and consider $0.99 until you can get the higher prices.

$2.99—Royalty of $1.05 (at 35%) or $2.09 (70% minus the download fee)

$2.99 is the baseline for most pricing. This is the lowest price point to get 70% royalties from Amazon (Amazon's limited Countdown Deals excepted). $2.99 to $9.99 is the window in which the majority of regular prices exist because Amazon has made it that way. We have to work within the system as it is, not as we want it to be. When you're a big enough name, you can lobby to change things, but for now, let's go with this $2.99 to $9.99 window.

When I started out, I priced my full-length books at $2.99 to maximize my royalties while still giving readers who were skeptical about the new guy a lower risk option to give my stuff a try. I priced all my books at $2.99, the first six or so, but then I raised prices when my traditional publisher (I have four books with a legacy group), listed my 50k-word books for $6.99. That series reached bestseller status at that price for the individual books.

They commanded the higher price because they had conditioned their readers to pay it. They were also wide, selling on all platforms. Still, the majority of their sales came from Amazon. Was my book worth $6.99 or $2.99? I tried pricing my self-published stuff higher, but that killed all my sales. I reduced the price to $3.99 as I wasn't a total newcomer. That worked. They were the brand and not this new guy from Alaska writing a post-apocalyptic survival book.

I still have a series starter or two at $2.99, but I sell as many of those as I do the ones at $4.99. Why? Perception of value. Any readers who pull up anything from me will find that I have a great number of books and they are almost all $4.99. Now, $2.99 looks like a bargain instead of something cheap.

I always say dress for the job you want. That means, you make your book look like it belongs where it is, from the attention-grabbing cover to the enticing one-click blurb, to the price that others in your genre are getting. Look at the below top eight in the Young Adult - Aliens category. You'll see my complete omnibus there for $4.99 which is the most common price. There are a couple sales for $0.99 and there's one book for $5.99, but that one is published by MacMillan (a Big Five publisher). Does that mean the book is better? Not in the least. It means they have more overhead and are spending far more on advertising to get where I am with almost no overhead and relatively minimal advertising.

This also has deviated from the conversation about the $2.99 price point. This top eight list illustrates how prices climb and where sales fit in the big scheme. Dress for the job you want—price your book competitively, without giving readers the opportunity to put your book down. Entice them to pick it up and keep reading.

Doing this kind of research is important to finding the right price point for your genre. Young Adult aliens, adventure, space opera, and military science fiction are all in my wheelhouse. I know what the top books are getting. The books on sale jump in and out of the top ten, but the stalwart performers with consistently high sales call for a certain price. That is my regular price, too. It just so happens to be $4.99.

I have three different series of novellas, twelve in one, nine in another, and eight in the last one. I price these novellas (my books are between 20k and 30k words) at $2.99. I think that's a fair price for a shorter book. Many readers agree. Some do not. I don't write these books for the people who don't agree. They are good stories.

$3.99 to $4.99—royalty of $1.40 to $3.49 (minus the download fee)

These are your value price points. High enough to make people double check, but not so high that potential readers are turned off before they look any further. My regular price on most of my books is $4.99. My usual download fee is about nine cents because my books don't have images within or anything that bumps up the size too much. That means I'm getting about $3.40 per sale.

The $4.99 price point is good for my genre—science fiction. Crime fiction calls for a higher price point—look at the top eight. Three are trade publications (trad pub), and the other five are Amazon imprints. Can you tell which three are trad? Pricing is all over the place, but to bust into the top ranks of crime fiction, you need to sell a lot of books.

At one point in time, Regency Romance books drew a high price. I just checked historical romance, all subgenres and the majority of titles in the top fifty are priced at $0.99. That's a tough nut to crack. To make money, you need to have a price that works to bring in enough revenue; otherwise, you are constantly pushing to sell big numbers. $0.35 vs $3.40. I need to sell one copy to earn the same as someone selling ten copies trapped at a $0.99 price point.

Think about that when you head into a genre (writing to market). You need readers willing to pay your price. Sometimes competition is good, other times, the competition will bury you. It's how Amazon built the goliath it has. Amazon sacrificed a significant amount to gain market share. Once Amazon dominated the marketplace, they started to dictate different terms. Amazon owns some 85% of the ebook market.

Once again, we work with the system we have. Understanding it is half the battle. After that, you have to figure out how it can best serve you. That's what this book is about. My $4.99 books help me make my mortgage payment, thanks to 70% royalties. My traditional publisher royalties, not so much.

$5.99 to $6.99—Royalty of $2.10 to $4.89 (minus the download fee).

I've tried $5.99 and $6.99. That was a big no-joy for me. As of October, 2019, $5.00 was the threshold beyond which sales of single books in science fiction did not happen. But look at that earning potential. Nearly $5 for every sale. The bottom line is I didn't get any sales, so 70% of nothing is...add naught to naught, carry the naught, double check the math, and it's still zero.

In crime fiction (or other sub-genres where prices are higher), you can drop a price of $5.99 or $6.99 to sit between the titles on sale and the titles from traditional publishers that are extreme (but from household name authors). James Patterson's books are at $14.99 for the ebook. A little pricey, but the publisher is trying to push the sale of the hardback because that's their business model and believe it or not, a higher profit margin than the ebook.

In the Fantasy category, Harry Potter ebooks are priced at $8.99 each. There are some truly massive Fantasy tomes and those are priced to $14.99 (from legacy publishing), but most fantasy books show up as $3.99 to $4.99. Weird. Fantasies are usually much longer books and even these lower priced offerings are weighing in at over 400 pages. The competition is healthy in the main Fantasy category, but I know many of those authors and they are doing quite well in the big scheme. Their strategic marketing campaigns are delivering market share (a core group of growing readership) with a sufficient royalty share.

For science fiction, $5.99 doesn't seem to be a happy place but I will eventually move all my books to that price point. Not this year, but maybe next especially as I gain new readers and continue to grow in popularity (not ego speaking, it's pure business—I have the social proof to go along with it, nearly five thousand five-star reviews on Amazon). And then I hope everyone comes along with me. Dress for the job you want.

I price some box sets and omnibuses of my shorter books, the ones I price at $2.99 individually, for $6.99 as a three-book box set. Buy three books for the price of two (almost). With all the advertising I've done, those campaigns don't resonate as much as a good campaign on Book 1. When the readers like the book because they are emotionally connected to the characters, they'll pick up Book 2.

$7.99 to $9.99—Royalties of $2.80 to $6.99 (minus download fee)

These price points are for established authors on single books or, in my case, omnibus editions. I'll bundle three or four books that individually go for $4.99 and price them at $9.99 because of Amazon's upper limit for a 70% royalty rate. Those bundles also have a huge number of pages. Anyone looking at the Amazon product page can see the page count. Print length of my complete set omnibus is 2,206 pages. That's an advertising quote all by itself—Over 2,200 pages for only $9.99.

Product details

File Size: 2919 KB
Print Length: 2206 pages
Simultaneous Device Usage: Unlimited
Publication Date: May 23, 2019
Sold by: Amazon Digital Services LLC
Language: English
ASIN: B0756CL35P
Text-to-Speech: Enabled
X-Ray: Not Enabled
Word Wise: Enabled
Lending: Enabled
Screen Reader: Supported
Enhanced Typesetting: Enabled
Amazon Best Sellers Rank: #9,012 Paid in Kindle Store (See Top 100 Paid in Kindle Store)
    #9 in Teen & Young Adult Alien Science Fiction
    #7 in Teen & Young Adult Aliens eBooks
    #28 in Science Fiction Anthologies (Books)

A sale of that beast earns $6.64, but it's in Kindle Unlimited and is at the price point where people might borrow it and read it. A full read is worth from $12 to $13.50 (depending on the payout rate for the month). That large of a book is a big win, even though if I sold all nine books separately at $4.99 each, the total earnings would be a whopping $30.54. These are all things to consider as part of your pricing and marketing model.

From a box set perspective, I don't usually box my books until they've been out for a year in order to maximize the individual book sales revenue before consolidating the books into a collection which generally appeals to a different readership or those readers who picked up the series in Kindle Unlimited and would like to re-read it without having to check out the books again. Having them in a single collection is appealing.

Higher than $9.99—(35% royalty rate with Amazon but a 70% rate with Kobo, B&N, & Apple)

When is your book able to warrant a price higher than $9.99? That is the magical question that I can only guess at. If you're James Patterson or another household name, then, you can command whatever price you want for your unique titles that the world must have. You're also an author who isn't reading this book because if you're a household name, you have people taking care of this stuff for you. In the indie world, it's just us.

But box sets that are massive should have no problem commanding a higher price. I have a ten-book series that is long, like 750k words long. I currently have it in two box sets. At some point, if I pull it from KU, then wide and higher royalties is a siren's call to higher profits, and with the new platforms comes an entirely new group of readers. Time is your friend. You can exploit Amazon's models and algorithm love (helping you sell books that are already selling), get your page reads, get your #1 New Release or Bestseller banner, then bounce wide with the series to maximize your exposure and profit. So many different ways to make money in this world. You just need to know the options.

Subscription Model (KDP Select, also known as Kindle Unlimited)

To get into KDP Select, you will commit to having your title exclusively with Amazon for a three-month period. The box to renew is automatically selected, so to end your participation, you have to manually uncheck the box after you're already participating to turn it off. Also note the date that it ends. Even if you unpublish your book, it is still exclusive to Amazon until that end date. This is where the three-month commitments come in handy. No matter what happens, it's only three months. But keep track. If you write in a series like me and have lots of books, you have books coming and going every single week. It helps to have a date that it went in, so you can do a quick calculation without having to pull up your KDP dashboard.

I live on my spreadsheets—I can do anything with them, but I digress.

The subscription model of pricing is difficult for the business-minded author to use in order to make sound decisions using better projections looking ahead. With Amazon's Kindle Edition Normalized Pages (KENP) pay rate, you don't find out what each page pays until fifteen days after the end of the month in which those page reads were earned.

What's a page read? Every book enrolled in KU has a page count (pull up your KDP dashboard, not your product page on regular Amazon—the page count listed there is not your page count for pay purposes, thank goodness because the product page number is almost always lower).

You find the information on your dashboard. Hover over the three dots on the far right side of your ebook listing. Select KDP Select. On this shot, you'll find that the box set was not in KDP Select and not available for reading in KU. So, I clicked "Enroll." That took me to the next screen and asked me to confirm. I confirmed and then it brought up the following to show that I was enrolled, what the dates were, and how many pages the book was worth.

Your Current KDP Select Status: Enrolled

Term start date: October 13, 2019 PDT
Term end date: January 10, 2020 PST

Manage KDP Select Enrollment

Run a Price Promotion

Sign your book up for a Kindle Countdown Deal or a Free Book Promotion. Only one promotion can be enabled per enrollment period.

Run an Ad Campaign

With Amazon Advertising, you set your budget, targeting, and timing. You pay only when shoppers click your ads. To create an ad campaign, choose the Amazon marketplace where you want the ad to appear. To advertise this book in multiple marketplaces, repeat this step for each marketplace. Learn more

◉ Kindle Countdown Deal Learn more ▾
◯ Free Book Promotion Learn more ▾

Choose a marketplace:

Choose... ▾

Create a new Kindle Countdown Deal

Create an ad campaign

You must select a marketplace where you would like to advertise your book from the drop-down menu above.

Earn royalties from the KDP Select Global Fund

Earn your share of the KDP Select Global Fund when customers read your books from Kindle Unlimited and the Kindle Owners' Lending Library. You'll be paid for each page individual customers read of your book, the first time they read it. To determine a book's page count in a way that works across genres and devices, we've developed the Kindle Edition Normalized Page Count (KENPC) v3.0. Learn more

"Cygnus Space Opera Books 1 to 3"

Kindle Edition Normalized Page Count (KENPC) v3.0: 1399

At the very bottom above is the KENPC. Cygnus Space Opera trilogy has 1399 pages.

How much will one read-through earn if you don't know the rate? We have a lot of historical data to better guesstimate what the rates will be. It generally goes up around October through December. It traditionally goes down in January through March, back up for a little, down for the summer, then starts climbing through to the end of the year where the rates are the highest.

Rates are generally around $0.0045 per page, going down as low as $0.004 or as high as $0.005. If you're risk averse, use the lower number for your projections. I had some five million page reads this past month. I'll use $0.0045 because it will be closer to reality than $0.004. That means I am projecting around $22,500 for KENP revenue with a worst-case low of $20,000 and best case high of $25,000. That's a significant range, but once again, I'll say that you have to work with the system as it is, not how you want it to be. It would be nice to know what you'll get paid as the page reads happen, just like a sale, but it doesn't. You have to use projections to budget.

You get the page-read counts as they happen as shown on your KDP dashboard reports page, but this is also an estimate. You may lose pages if Amazon determines they came from a non-credible source. Scammers have been bilking millions from the system by faking page read numbers through server farms and real accounts, but the books aren't being read, just signed out and skimmed. Just like the game Whack-a-Mole, every time Amazon knocks one down, two more pop up. If you suddenly go from five million page reads to three million, don't blame Amazon, blame the scammers. And then follow up with an email to Amazon just to make sure there wasn't a mistake.

Here's where pricing comes into play. My books are generally around 60,000 words. Depending on unknown factors, the normalized pages go anywhere from 280 to 350. Whatever you do, don't add line spacing and extraneous characters trying to increase your page count. If Amazon catches you trying to artificially increase your pages, you'll be removed and banned from the platform that accounts for 85% of all book sales. You don't want to do that to your career. Accept your page count, unless it seems way too low or way too high, and then you can request a manual review.

So your 60k-word book priced at $4.99 can earn you, through the subscription service, an estimated $1.26 to $1.58 per copy. A $4.99 book sale can earn you roughly $3.40 (assuming a $0.09 download fee, which is average). Why don't we all just sell our books instead?

There's the rub. The subscription service makes it possible for high-volume readers to get their money's worth at a low cost. It's just like Netflix. How many movies or shows have you streamed for your one low fee? Would you have bought those same shows? I have to because I can't stream where I live, so I'm far more discriminating in what I buy. And that is exactly where your readers are. There will be some overlap between readers who buy and readers who subscribe, but it's not enough for me to jump out of the subscription service. I feel for the people who are on limited income, so they read instead of watching the more expensive TV. Kindle makes cheap reads possible, and these folks devour books. I want them in my corner.

And then I box up the sets after a certain amount of time and ask my readers if it's time for a re-read. Although box sets earn you page reads, they don't earn you an Amazon all-star bonus that you might get with an individual title. I'm good with that, as Amazon has stated clearly that they wouldn't include box sets or omnibuses in the all-star bonus running because it is simply a repackaging of other titles. If you've only published an omnibus edition without publishing the individual titles, then Amazon's prohibition against being eligible for an all-star bonus doesn't apply. I discuss this strategy later in the subsection on box sets.

For a consolidation of individual titles, I don't mind getting paid twice for almost no extra work. I don't have to write a new book to get paid like I did—and then some. BUT, you do have to have all participating titles exclusive to Amazon in order to bundle them and put them in KU. You cannot have individual titles wide and the box set in KU. It doesn't work that way (or vice versa).

When I checked things for this KU section, I saw that my Free Trader 1-9 omnibus was at 2,940 pages. Amazon won't pay above 3,000 pages in a single volume (thank the scammers for that rule), so I'm happy not to be over. My omni used to be 2,964 pages, and it had a download fee of $0.49. I had the book covers in there for each book in the series. I took them out by deleting ten pages. Deleting ten pages of images reduced my page count by 24. Wait a minute! Yet, it also reduced my download fee to $0.35. It cost me an estimated $0.11 and saved me $0.15. I gained four cents per copy for buyers over readers. It's a win for my bottom line as I'm about evenly split in revenue between page reads and purchases.

I have nearly all my titles in KU because, for me and my genre, it makes sense. A huge swath of science fiction readers are ready for the next title. I only need to show them it's there —newsletter, advertising, and promotions to celebrate the newest release, book one is only 99 cents!

Fantasy and romance do well wide. You have to research for your genre, but there are people who are more up on it, like Draft2Digital and K-Lytics.

Some people are deathly afraid Amazon will cancel their account and leave them hanging. The reason people think about it is because those who have lost their accounts were the most vocal. They represent a fraction of a percent of those who publish on Amazon. I'm not worried because I have all aspects in my control, such as no extra spacing, no bonus books to bump up the page count, nothing shady or even shady looking.

I'm not going to worry about hypotheticals. I'm going to figure out how to find more readers and reap what I sow.

CHAPTER THREE

What are those prices

- Pre-order price
- Regular price
- Sale price
- How to put a book on sale
- Promotions
- The perception of value
- The value of free
- The $0.99 sale
- The KU impact on sales
- Other sale prices
- Calculating read-through/buy-through

There are three revenue pillars that your book can establish. The regular price, the sale price, and the secondary format (audio and paperback).

. . .

Pre-order price

Pre-orders are another tool in the author toolbox. You can list your title, show your cover (or even a placeholder) and secure your publication date up to a year in advance.

Important safety tip when it comes to pre-orders: If you lower the price at any point during the pre-order period, every sale comes at that lowest price. If you had a thousand pre-orders at full price, $4.99 and you dropped the price to $0.99 too early as you tried to get that purchase spike during launch week, instead of $3400 in revenue on launch day, you'll be getting $350.

Don't do that unless you meant to. And still, that's not optimal. Who wants to lose thousands of dollars? Also, don't panic if you aren't getting swarms flocking to your pre-order. Many people won't buy a book on pre-order and usually not from an author they don't know. It's a big risk. If they wait until the book is published, they can read the sample through the Look Ahead feature or they can borrow it, if it is in KU, or they can buy it at that time based on whatever criteria is important to that reader. You never know what might hold them back. Price usually is not the reason, unless you've already trained your readers to expect your books at a lower price. Then you'll need to go through a bit of wailing and gnashing of teeth before they settle into your new pricing scheme.

I generally price my pre-orders at either regular price or one dollar less than regular price, a single title at $4.99 or $3.99. If the book were a novella, I would price it at $2.99 to take advantage of that sweet 70% royalty. If I had it wide, I'd still price the book at that.

When a person buys a book on pre-order, your book gets rank credit at that time, but you don't get the revenue from the sale until it goes live. And when it goes live, your KU readers will jump in and borrow it. You will get additional rank credit from your pre-orders, but it is a fraction of the pre-order numbers. Whether it's thirty pre-orders to get rank credit for one sale or ten, no one outside of Amazon knows. And rank is good for visibility only if you get the sales and borrows to go along with it.

We all look for that magical place known as "sticky." It's where your book hits a certain high rank and then stays there without pouring additional money into advertising. It's no secret that Amazon likes making money. If you have a product that is already making money, they'll jump on the mini-bandwagon and give it a little extra nudge. With their horsepower, that extra nudge goes a long way. This is why you tend to see the same people at the top of the charts. Amazon likes winners. But, don't despair. We all started somewhere other than at the top.

Pre-orders also guarantee your publication date. If you upload a title and press "I'm ready to publish now," the book could go live up to three days later. I've seen one extreme case of eleven days before an anthology went live because one of the short stories had been previously published.

Amazon supports pre-orders up to one year out. You can set it up and let it roll. Don't forget, as you don't want to lose your pre-order rights, but you can move your publication date up to one month later in case you're not ready.

All of that has to do with the reader experience. Amazon puts their customers first. Pre-orders are good because they guarantee a midnight download. They let authors work up the publication frenzy. And they let authors slip a month as preferable than canceling completely (that leads to a worse reader experience than a delay).

Pre-orders give you the link to set up release swaps and promotions. Without a pre-order, you must wait until the book is live before sharing the link. This could be prohibitive in getting a paid promotion.

Here's a secret tip for books in KU with the potential to earn one of those coveted monthly bonuses. End your pre-order (as in publish your book) on the last day of the month so you get paid that good pre-order money in roughly sixty days. And, then, you have the full month to earn max page reads to compete for the KU all-star bonus. That bonus could mean a $500 to $25,000 kicker to your earnings. Plus, it's a cash flow coup. End the pre-order one day later and you won't get paid for an extra month, nearly 90 days from the big earning day until that money is in your bank. Get the best of both worlds. Set up your pre-order to end on a date that benefits you.

Regular price (aka full price)

Woohoo! Regular price is where you train your readers regarding your book's commercial value. As an author, ignore the time and money you put into a book and look at what the market will bear. I would love my books to be priced at $99.99 because I put in the time to learn the craft and pound out a compelling tale with an awe-inspiring cover. No one cares what's behind the scenes. They only care what they see on the bookshelf. What makes your book stand out? Don't let it be the price. If a buyer looks at ten books and nine of them are at $4.99, he/she will look further to figure out which one to pick up. If there's a title at $0.99, the reader might pick it up first (that's what discounted promotions are all about). For the books that are a comparable price, other things will draw the eye—this is why you need a genre appropriate cover that pulls people in.

This applies to Book 1 as much as Book 15 in your series. It applies to your standalones. It has taken me a while to train my readership since I started out at $2.99. My full-length novels are $4.99 now. Get them used to the regular price point and incentivize that for them. Like giving them access to the book for a full month before you run your first promotion. Time has a value. Exclusivity has a value. Special incentives for those who pay full price to make them feel unique.

It's the value proposition. Do readers feel they are getting value from your book? Of course, when they are wondrously entertained, they will be waiting for the next volume. But what about before they are fans? You have to hook them and make them feel special. "This book will never be priced at $3.99 again!" or "Tomorrow it goes up to full price. Get it now."

Full price lets you do that. Advertising for a book at full price should hit readers who are looking for a great read and not looking to just snag a bargain. You are buying their valuable time, and they are paying you for the pleasure, so you better write a good book—readers vote with their money.

Get your regular price correct, because this is the standard you are setting, the baseline from which everything else flows. Pricing your book higher over time makes early buyers happy while discounting your book makes early buyers sad (if it's too close to their purchase date). I've told people that a discount was coming up in the hopes that my fans would start sharing the news. It crushed my regular price sales. When you discount your stuff, drop it on your readers like a happy surprise. "I'm just as surprised as you are that this book is now ninety-nine cents!"

Even if they didn't believe me, at least no one balked.

Your regular (full) price is what the market will bear, which means, what your genre will support. In some, it's $6.99, others, $9.99. Don't be fooled by all the ebooks listed at $14.99. Those are from traditional publishers who have a completely different methodology to engage readers. Many readers won't pay that. They'll buy the hardback instead, which is exactly what the $14.99 price point is meant to do. The authors are fan favorites, stalwarts in the industry, because the legacy publishers and their supporting infrastructure have told you they are. And the readers are fans of their stories. I can't denigrate the big numbers that top authors generate, but exclusivity is something that has a value. If the only way you can get your favorite author's latest book is by paying $14.99, then so be it, but you've been groomed for a long time before you hit that point.

Indies generally don't have that kind of horsepower or overhead to demand such a price point. Amazon has determined our optimal pricing is between $2.99 and $9.99. They've done the market research and that's why they incentivize this price range. I trust that they know what they're doing. My revenue suggests they do. They trust I know what I'm doing when they give my books an extra boost, and we're both rewarded with additional sales of this book and others, too.

Where do I advertise my stuff at regular (i.e. full) price? I use Amazon Advertising and Facebook Ads. These take some trial and error in targeting to dial in the most receptive readers. The broader you go, the more you'll spend while (probably) making fewer sales. You want to zero in your target audience, then slowly expand. You'll know once you are getting readers who aren't fans. That's where reading your reviews is important. When you get a review that starts with "I thought I was getting...," then you've gone where you don't want to go. Dial it back and expand somewhere else. Always tinkering with your full-price ads is important, because this is going to be the bulk of your consistent revenue, while sales will give you some nice revenue spikes and maybe even a burgeoning KU tail.

Sale price

- How to put a book on sale & the physical value of sales price
- Promotions
- Perception of value
- The value of Free
- The $0.99 sale
- KU impact on sales
- Other sale prices

A sale price is the discount from your regular price. It is a part of your marketing strategy to bring new readers on board. In my case, I also discount every new release for one day, a week after publication to reward my most loyal readership, but that will evolve to once a month to not at all.

It can also be referred to as a loss leader, meaning that you expect to lose money on it but are counting on buyers to get into your other products, turning it into a long-term win. That's what it means to be in the long game. Marketing is all about bringing more readers on board. That simple and that hard. Are you targeting the right readers in the right way? Is your cover catching their eye, in a good way? Does your blurb make them click the buy button? And, then, does your story make them want to read more of your work?

Market the holy hell out of your books, intelligently, to gain buyers who will like your style. That's it, but that's not what this book is about. This book is about getting the most from your pricing, and sales prices can cost you a lot of money if you price too low, or they can cost you leads if you price too high. Let's start at the high end.

I've run a huge amount of one -dollar-off sales—$3.99 instead of my regular price of $4.99—and I think that is a significant waste of time. I'm not sure it draws any additional sales on top of what I'm already getting. I don't think a 20% discount when it comes to an ebook is compelling. 50% or more is the ticket with 80% as the sweet spot. I don't have hard data to support that, but here's what I see.

A regular priced book of $4.99 doesn't necessarily sell well when discounted to $2.99. We (the collective community) have conditioned readers to expect single book sales to be at $0.99. That is slowly creeping up as many are now discounted to $1.99, which is still more than 50% off a $4.99 title. Some big-name authors are discounting to $2.99, but these are legacy published for $9.99 or more which means a discount of at least 70%. Everyone loves the big number, but many forget that it was grossly overpriced to begin with. That's how most discount stores work. Half off a ridiculously high price may still be too high.

Don't overprice your book, but don't underprice it either. What is appropriate for your genre? For some, that number is $2.99, others $4.99, and some are even $9.99 (niche with a small audience and too few offerings—it's the golden rule of supply and demand). If you are in an underserved genre and you have the best book there, all you have to do is tell people about it (advertise and promote) and you'll sell it at full price. Other times, you have to vault past the group to wave your book in front of the potential readers.

I would try $0.99 before I tried Free with a book's first marketing campaign.

$0.99 is a common sale point and brings some ownership to the reader. They spent a buck and are more likely to read it.

For every sale, you get $0.35 rather than nothing. You'll move fewer copies when you have it for $0.99, but total numbers don't matter if no one reads your book. At least you're getting something while you're impatiently waiting for your book to climb to the top of someone's TBR pile.

$0.99 is far and away the most popular sale price, regardless of genre. $1.99 gets fewer sales but this price point is becoming more and more common. Recently, in my BookBub reader newsletter, most sale prices were $1.99. They cost more, but you only need half the number of sales to make the same money. Enticing? The readers decide with their money. Look at the top 100 list of your genre, then look at it tomorrow because it will have changed, and then the next day, too. Study and learn. This is your business! Don't half-ass what could be the most lucrative career of your life.

How to put a book on sale

On Amazon, you might have two choices. If you are in KU, you can run a Countdown Deal. Go to your KDP bookshelf, click on Promote and Advertise. That takes you to a page where you can setup a free run (five days a quarter) or a Countdown Deal (seven days, starting at least thirty days after your last price change and ending at least fourteen days before the end of your KDP quarter). You can select two increments. I double checked on a book priced $2.99 (I had just changed the price to run a promotion, so the CD wasn't available for another twenty-eight days), and the suggested increments were $0.99 to start and then $1.99 to wrap before returning to the regular price.

When would you do a multiple increment Countdown Deal? When you are testing promotional sites and various newsletters. If you can get $1.99, why wouldn't you want to get that as a CD and earn $1.40 in royalties instead of being strapped to the idea that you have to always reduce your books to $0.99 for a sale?

If you are not in KU, then you must change the price manually. If you are reducing the price to anything below $2.99, you'll have to change the royalty rate to 35% (but you won't be charged a download fee). If you are with an aggregator like Draft2Digital, you can use their slick one-time pricing tool for a discount promotion. You set the date you want to start, the date you want to end, and the price. They do all the rest and make it easy. And with Draft2Digital, you get an effective 60% royalty on all sales. Not bad at all.

If you are direct with Apple, B&N, and Kobo, you'll need to go to each site and change the price. It doesn't take long. The big challenge is if you are wide and trying to promote a book for free. You'll change your other distributors to zero and then ask Amazon to price match. They may not do it as quickly as you like, so you'll need to give yourself some lead-time to make sure everything is in place by the time your paid promotions and newsletter swaps run.

Promotions

Promotions are kings when it comes to sale prices. You can hit paid promotional newsletters like Ereader News Today (ENT), BargainBooksy, BookBarbarian, and so many more. 20Booksto50k® has a couple different lists in the Files section of general sites that have worked for people and they include genre. I Love Vampire Network (ILVN) caters to paranormal (vampires) and there is Red Roses Romance for titles in that genre. There are many different options, but you have to search to find them. There are free sites (like Book Hippo out of the UK) and Free99Books, so it doesn't hurt to list a discounted book with them if you can get a slot.

Manage your promotions two months out. Book Thanksgiving and Christmas as early as possible (some sites don't open until two months or less before the promo date, so be aware; others sell out three months in advance for the choice dates like Black Friday or Cyber Monday). Early bird gets the worm, right?

You can try to swap newsletters with other authors in your genre. Reach for the sky but keep your feet on the ground. There are some big name authors out there who promote newer folks, but your quality must be up there. The bigger names don't want to risk losing their own subscribers because of showing a sub-standard book. But you also should be confident your work is good as authors are usually the worst judge of their own stuff. Find out what strangers think, and make sure they are strangers who read your genre (remember, genre = marketing). Don't argue with readers who tell you they think your book is a mystery and not a thriller. If you hear it more than once, then you might want to consider looking at audiences in that genre and test some readers over there.

The right genre is the one where you will find the most readers who like your book. It absolutely doesn't matter what you think it is. It only matters how the readers receive it. I usually promote in more than one genre in order to see how it resonates. After over a hundred books, though, I don't stretch those wings too far into the unknown. I know what my readers like, and I do my best to give it to them, more of the same, but different. It stays exciting for me with new plot points, different ways of looking at things, but the good guys will win in the end.

How do you get the most from a discounted book?

Set up as many promotions as you can afford to tap as

many new readers as possible. Each promotion is designed to bring new readers into the world of "you." If you have one series, then it's the series you are trying to sell. For me, I have sixteen different series and growing, so I'm trying to get new readers to look at me as the brand and then sell them all sixteen series.

In either case, you want them to buy the first one. A way to do that is at a discount (low risk) and then the new readers fall in love with your words. You can influence whether the readers fall in love with you (I have a book called *Write Compelling Fiction* that can help you), but you can't control it. You can control putting the book before them, and that's what promotions are all about.

Stack your promotions over the course of a few days, light on the first day, just in case there's an issue with your price, you don't lose all your money or irk potential buyers who think you pulled a bait and switch. Go heavy on the middle days. Then, light again on the last day to clean up those who don't check their email daily. If they click two days after they received it, most will understand that the discount was time limited.

There will always be outlier readers who think it should be on sale whenever they click. You can't do anything about them, although for customers in the US, I've gifted them copies. I get the royalty, so it means minimal cost. For a $4.99 book, that costs me a buck and a half, effectively, and I might gain a new reader. They took the time to contact me and were willing to spring a dollar for the book. I'll give them a chance to put up or shut up. I've never had one contact me after the first book to ask for another free one. I have had a couple contact me to tell me they were buying the rest of the series.

Treat your customers well. Weed out those who want a

free ride and embrace the rest, then find more like those in the latter group.

When running a sale, make sure you keep it to a limited time. Don't drop the price and just leave it there.

Unless your sales suggest you should.

There are no absolutes. I had my box set at $9.99. For nine books, that's a good deal and I was getting sales. I put up my best ad ever on Facebook and mentioned $9.99 in the ad itself. I let it run when I dropped the price to $1.99, then $2.99, and finally $4.99. I have not yet changed the price back to $9.99 because I'm getting a positive ROI of two to three to one every single day with it as is. Since this omnibus is less than ten percent of my inventory of books, I can leave it as is. I'm not cutting off my nose to spite my face.

I will change it back to $9.99 at some point and, after six months I'll probably drop the price and run a limited discount again. My conversion of the clicks to buys on my Facebook ad is high, because if someone is willing to pay $9.99, and then they get to Amazon to see it's only $4.99, that's an easy one-click.

The perception of value

Even at a discounted price, books have perceived value. 80% off sounds like a great deal ($0.99 versus your regular price of $4.99). For an omnibus edition, that's priced at $9.99, a discount to $2.99 is 67% off the regular price. The regular price is the standard by which your book will be judged versus what a reader is willing to pay for a book from an author they don't know. I'm assuming these are new readers because you should have established your price baseline with your existing readership with your first book or an updated pricing strategy once you became more established.

I cannot overstate the importance of researching your genre, the one where your readers are located, not the one you might think you belong. Hopefully these overlap to reduce extra stress in your life. The prices of books in that genre are the bellwether in your pricing strategy. Remember, dress for the job you want.

Show up strong. I don't mean you need to price your books at three dollars more than everyone else so you look more important. That might work. I'll have to try it someday, but I don't want to blow a lot of money on it. I know what I would think of the outlier. I wouldn't give it a second glance. When I see ebooks priced at $14.99, my instant thought is that's legacy publishing trying to get you to buy the hardback. I don't necessarily look at price first, but $14.99 for an ebook is a non-starter for me. I'm sure there are plenty of people who pay it because they are under the misperception that there is no one better than the author they selected. There are plenty who are just as good, if they only give them a chance and that's what marketing and promotions are all about.

Someone who gives you a shot at $0.99, might be willing to pay $14.99 for your ebook once they become a superfan. Value is earned, not given.

The perception of value on the other hand? This is why you have genre appropriate covers in the highest quality, whether you do it yourself or have someone else do it. You don't want to be the only one in blue jeans and a t-shirt when everyone else is wearing a suit, at least not until you're the one who can establish trends. Be that person eventually, but no one starts there unless they have another edge. You have to get in the door before you can influence what's inside.

You want the instant perception of your book to be positive. Cover, blurb, and first chapter. I've tried reading a lot of books. I've talked with a great number of indies. If you have to tell a reader, "keep reading, it gets better," you've already lost them. Mickey Spillane said it best with "The first chapter sells this book, and the last chapter sells the next one."

Wise words. You may market the hell out of your book and move big numbers of copies, but if no one goes on to the next one, there is a fundamental problem with your book. With your business hat on, you need to get feedback and figure it out, then fix it. No pricing strategy will make you money over the long term if your first book isn't gripping readers.

Yes, you're reading a book on pricing strategies, and I'm talking about the quality of your first book. You can put the most expensive lipstick on a pig, and it'll still be a pig. But if you put that shade of gloss on a Ferrari...

Have you seen Ferrari or Bentley ads? They are focused on invite-only, high-end clientele. Bentley spent $372k in 1997. That's almost nothing. Why? Their customers are already on board. They are on the Bentley mailing list. When you see authors talking about making a great deal of money with little advertising, they are the Ferraris and Bentleys of publishing. Their newsletter lists have people who will buy their product. They guard these lists like Fort Knox, not often sharing another author's title. When asked about a tagline, Ferrari responded with. "Ferrari is its own tagline."

That's what branding looks like. And that's when you can charge almost whatever you like for your ebook. I saw a number one bestseller on all of Amazon. It was simply "New novel by John Grisham." That was it—a black cover with white text. No book title, no blurb, just the promise of another Grisham novel.

Between the start and that point, however, you need to bring those readers on board, build your Ferrari notification list. A $0.99 sale will bring you those folks willing to take a look. It's like paying to take a test drive, but a pittance, just enough to show that you might be serious. Don't discount the ninety-nine centers. These are good people who just put $0.35 into your pocket. They are paying you for the pleasure of giving your book a shot. Their standards will be high, but if you can win them over, then you add one more name to your Ferrari list. These are the people who sign up from the back of your books because they like what they read, also known as organic subscribers. Make sure you keep your organic subscribers list separate from all of your other newsletter subscribers.

You don't want to send ads for a Chevy Vega to your Ferrari customers. You want them to pay your full price for the benefit of dealing directly with the author on matters of import to them (like getting your next book on release day).

The value of Free

Dropping the price of your book to Free. I do it. Think of it as the free samples at the grocery store. What if you got a free sample, but they didn't have any product for sale? By the time you leave the store, you've forgotten what that product was, even if it was one of the best things you ever tasted.

And that's why I strongly discourage people from giving their book away for free if they don't have any other books available, but that doesn't apply if you are using it as a reader magnet, a way to get someone's email address to join your newsletter. In that case, you're not giving the book away for free. The price is their email address. Your free book should be every bit as good as anything else you have because you want to sell a skeptical new reader on your product. You want to convince them to invest their reading time in you.

So, don't half-ass this. Still, if you make a misstep, you can recover. Put out a new book, a better book. Put on a new cover.

Fix the typos. Fix your prose. Fix your approach. It's all fixable. That's the power of being self-published. You don't have to worry about being rejected by a publisher. Go find new readers. Starting over isn't the same as re-rolling a title because you know what not to do. You learned a great deal that will help you improve the next time. What did Thomas Edison say? "I have successfully discovered 1,000 ways *not* to make a light bulb."

Free is a viable sale price. I might put my book for free a few months after I've floated it for sale at $0.99. Don't make it Free too quickly after publication as that cheapens the value of your work (probably—there are always exceptions). You don't want to drive away those folks who paid regular price. Don't panic. Put on your business hat and understand the sales principal of free samples.

You must have product for the readers to buy. Many will feel an obligation to pay for something because you have given them something. It is natural to feel that way. Have you bought something in a store simply because you used their bathroom? If you haven't and didn't feel guilty about it, you are in the minority. The group that free samples target are those who feel they owe you something. The anonymity of the internet makes it more likely that downloaders won't feel compelled to give any of your other work a try as a counter to looking someone in the face who just handed you a free sample. That's why the sample people fill the aisles in Costco on Saturday.

There's also a great deal of free and discounted samples out there. A person can download a hundred a day if they want. Their to-be-read (TBR) pile could be thousands of books strong. Digital books make that not just possible, but probable and a definite maybe in the likelihood of comprehensibility.

I'm not getting paid by the word despite that ridiculous

last sentence, but I wanted to poke fun at things we accept as truth. I believe that free comes with an implied string. I have some data to back it up, but I didn't even bother looking for a definitive study because I don't need to. I know that if ten people download my book for free, it's a win if one actually reads it. Those are numbers that I have personally seen. Ten percent is good and as more and more people put books out for free, five percent or even two percent could be a good read-through/buy-through. In some things, it is a numbers game.

For books set to Free, you want as many as possible downloaded, hopefully within the best genre for your title. There is significant risk if you put it in a genre where it doesn't belong. Half of my one-star reviews are from people who had no business downloading my book. It wasn't for them. They should have quit reading after the first page, but they didn't. They kept going far enough to feel morally justified in leaving that one-star review. It's the risk you take with Free, and something that you have to accept when you are marketing your book far and wide.

Not everyone is going to like it. But at least some of them will have tried it.

BookBub Featured Deals, the current gold standard of paid promotions, rely on read-through/sell-through to earn out, at least earn what you spent. The days of making tens of thousands of dollars from a BB feature with a two-month long tail are long past. If you can't earn back the cost of your Free promotion in two weeks, rethinking your pricing strategy is critical. Maybe that promotion would have earned better at $0.99.

A Free BookBub Featured Deal (both US and International) could cost you $500 (every genre is different). At that price, you need to sell 143 copies of a full-price book. That isn't that daunting, but it's not a given. If ten percent buy your next book, then that means you only need to give away 1,430 copies. If two percent (this is more likely the number unless your book is killer), then you'll need to give away 7,150 copies. These numbers are not absolute, they are only used to illustrate how the calculations work.

A BookBub Featured Deal, both US and International, should garner you that many copies. If the feature is cheaper, that's fewer number of copies you need people to download. Free is a numbers game, just like $0.99 when you put it on sale. You want the most in order to make the most money, but how many promotions do you need to get to the numbers you want in order to break even? If you keep spending, you may never break even.

It's called the law of diminishing returns, and Reedsy did a study on BookBub Free features. They determined that people who download Free books on BookBub are already members of most of the other paid promotion sites. Stacking your ads (at additional cost—FreeBooksy is $70 to run a one-time ad) may not earn you enough to get your money back. $70 at two percent buy-through means you need at least an additional 2,000 downloads.

If you have three or more books in a series (more is better), then free could bring you new readers. How much that is worth depends on the size of your backlist. If you only have two or three titles published, the answer is that it won't be worth as much as when you have ten titles to your name. The math is fairly simple regarding read-through/buy-through. For me, if I can get a reader to the third book in a series, they will usually end up reading the whole series. That's why that first three-book box set is such an attractive sale item, not necessarily for Free, but for sale.

. . .

The $0.99 sale

$0.99 is a common sale point and brings some ownership to the reader. They spent a buck and are more likely to read it.

Let's return to the calculations of a BookBub Featured Deal. If you get the US and International together for a title on sale for $0.99, you might pay $850 (this is about what it was for my last science fiction feature; again, every genre is different). At $850, you need to sell 2,429 copies at a 35% royalty rate and 1,417 copies at an effective rate of 60% (if you are wide through Draft2Digital for example) or 1,215 copies if you do a Countdown Deal and limit your Feature to just the US and UK. You cannot currently combine an Amazon Countdown Deal with a price drop for non-participating countries. You will get 35% royalties from Amazon to get all the countries for the Feature.

Can you move 2,429 copies? Probably. BookBub would not have selected your title if your cover wasn't enticing or your blurb information was off, even though they will rewicker your blurb, probably making it better because they know their readers. But that number is a minimum just to break even. Stacking ads by running a $0.99 sale across multiple sites, platforms, friends, and as many places as possible is important. One rule of sales is that a potential customer has to see something seven times before they respond. I have no idea how true it is, but if I keep seeing the same thing and it's in my genre, I will eventually pick it up.

Stacking those ads across a week or two weeks is important so Amazon gives you some love. They help sell books that are selling well. Amazon is not a big fan of spikes, a huge surge of sales in one day. I believe their system calculates a running seven-day/thirty-day average to see which books they show to potential customers. Amazon is all about making the sale. They are going to take as little risk in the process as possible, and that's why they don't just promote books for no reason. There is a reason, and it's based on past performance as an indicator of future potential. Unlike your stock purchases where you get that disclaimer.

Books are different. If a book is selling a little bit better each day, people take notice. A slow and steady climb up the charts will reward you more than a single day of the exact same number of sales. Do I have data to support this? Kind of, but it is an educated guess based on hundreds of examples. Some do better than others, and those are from consistent sales over a longer term. Single spikes die a quick death; although the revenue from that single spike usually pays for itself, then we wait to see what buy-through/read-through looks like.

This is the challenge—do you press forward with an advertising campaign without solid data saying your book has found traction? Is it part of your overall strategy? What is your budget? Don't lose your mind and start throwing money at something without being able to quantify the return. If your book has died on the vine, you're only donating to someone else's bottom line. Don't do that unless it also bolsters your own.

If you're getting no read-through/buy-through, then there may be a fundamental issue with the first book, and I'm not talking cover and blurb. I'm talking a story that the readers don't want to keep reading. Study your data and listen to what it tells you. You don't even need to dissect it.

You need to have some statistically significant numbers. If you run a promotion and you only sold two copies, then the data may not be sufficient to give you a read-through/buy-through rate. It could look like zero. If you've sold ten copies at $0.99, you're looking for a 50% read-through/buy-through. That could be three to seven copies of your second book that sell within the next two weeks. If you sell one hundred, then you should see better numbers that will give you the answers you're looking for. Is your story viable? Is your book good enough?

What about running a Countdown Deal where you earn 70% in both US and UK markets? Here's some timing to keep in mind—directly from Amazon. "Title has been enrolled in KDP Select for at least 30 days. Digital list price is unchanged for 30 days before or 14 days after your Kindle Countdown Deal runs." When you setup your Countdown Deal, understand thirty days before and two weeks after are untouchable for other price changes.

With one hundred copies out the door at $0.99, you want to see fifty sales of the second book, assuming its regular price is normal for the genre. Anything north of fifty is gravy. Anything south of twenty books with one hundred sales of book one should set off a few alarms. Those numbers are, once again, for illustrative purposes. The more purchases and the more downloads you get, the better your data will be. If your numbers suck, there's one of two issues:

1. You targeted the wrong readers (adjust and try again)
2. There's something wrong with your book (take a dispassionate look and fix it)

$0.99 sales are a great way to collect data from people willing to pay you for the pleasure. I see it as the new Free. I am not a fan of Free because of the overwhelming availability of books that people have made Free. I much prefer a marketing campaign based on less than a buck. But there are other ways to make money off ads besides the $0.99 sale.

. . .

KU impact on sales

But what about KU? This is where you have to take your best guesstimates based on book rank and then on pages read, where you have to assume that everyone reads to the last page. If the book is a hundred pages long (KENP count pages) and you have 1,000 pages read, you calculated ten books. It might be one hundred people reading only ten pages. You can't know for sure, except when it's borrowed. I built this chart based on my experience with more than one hundred books (and with assistance from Michael Anderle when it comes to the ranks inside 100).

Kindle Rank	Estimate of Books Sold & Borrowed in One Day	Daily Sales & Borrows to Maintain Rank
1	5000	5000
5	3500	2500
10	2500	2000
50	1500	1000
100	1000	500
200	500	300
1000	200	100
2500	100	50
5000	75	25
10,000	50	15
50,000	2	2
100,000	1	1

I include this chart to help you make your rough calculations. If your book hit a rank of 1,000 (congratulations!) but you only have one hundred sales, then you might have had about one hundred borrows. The book stays at 1,000 for three days. In days two and three, you sold only fifty books each day. You can assume that fifty were borrowed as well (assuming that's what your historical rate of borrows to buys has been. If you know yours, use that instead to guesstimate total numbers). Over the next week to two weeks, you should start seeing those page reads appear in your KDP dashboard. You can drill down to just the one book and it will tell you the exact number of page reads each day attributed to the book. Divide that number by the KENPC, one hundred in this case, and you'll have your estimated books read (for read-through purposes).

In my case, my KU revenue is nearly two to one compared to sales. Consequently, there is more value in longer books, at least the first in the series since everyone reads the first book, "everyone" being those who bought it based on your marketing efforts for a first in series or standalone. Know what you're shooting for. A $3.99 title needs to have 673 KENP to earn the same for a borrow and full read in KU versus a sale (70% royalty and $0.10 download fee). That's a pretty hefty book, about 120k-130k words. $4.99 is even more. That's how earnings work in the KU environment.

When you list a book for Free with Amazon, the default button is to borrow it in KU. Many people accidentally click this button instead of the Buy for $0.00 button (which takes two clicks, vice one-click for the Read for Free button).

In many cases, KU reads on a book will be worth far more than what you earn with a $0.99 sale and it's almost like free money if you offered your book for Free, but the reader borrowed it in KU instead. Some do that on purpose to help an author out while others do it by mistake. In either case, page reads earned because of a Free promotion are a bonus. You should never count on them. You want the readers to dig into your other stuff so any way a reader reads the first book is a good way. Sometimes you don't get paid and other times you do. The real payday is when they start picking up your other books.

That is always the goal. Don't be narrow-minded in hoping for a big score with one book. You won't know for a couple weeks how much they liked your book until they start getting into the others. If you can earn a 90% read-through/buy-through, then you'll know you have a great book.

Other sale prices

Assuming $0.35 for a 99-cent sale versus $0.70 for a $1.99 sale. Can you get at least half the number of sales of the $0.99 vs $1.99? If the answer is no, the lower price point (not free) could be an option to bring those traditional readers to you who don't want to risk that extra dollar on someone they don't know. Most readers have no idea that someone is self-published or working with a legacy publishing house.

BookBub Featured Deals are showing a great number of books at $1.99 or $2.99. A $2.99 ebook means that the book is at least $5.99 regular price. Many people who subscribe to BookBub won't buy a single book at $2.99, but they will buy a box set. My own data shows this to be true. But the costs of a $2.99 BookBub feature in my genre was $1,500. Ouch. In my nine-book omnibus, I earn $1.75 per copy sold because of the $0.35 download fee subtracted from the 70% royalty. That means I need to sell 857 copies to break even. At $0.99, I need to move 2,429 copies, but in my big omnibus, the lowest I could price it because of its size was $1.99. More cost to advertise, fewer sales to those browsing the bargain bins looking for a new author who might tickle their fancy.

Risk versus reward. I would not put a single title on sale for $2.99 unless I was at household name status, and then the book I put on sale would be ten years old. But that's what brand will do for you. Without that brand status, your discount prices may have to be lower, like $0.99 and for a box set/omnibus edition, maybe $0.99 or maybe $2.99. I don't go lower than $2.99 anymore, less than a dollar a book for a three or four-book set.

Dress for the job you want and build your brand to the point where the readers may have heard of you. That is what I'm counting on for my box set sales at higher prices than most of the other authors in my genre. As of writing this, I've spent more than two and a half years in the Amazon Top 100 for science fiction. That has earned me some name recognition. I'm going to try and leverage that. Otherwise, I'd be putting my box sets for $0.99, as much as it pained me to do so, unless I couldn't, as I found out with my monster nine-book box. And that's when the data glittered and sparkled before me.

And that nine-book omnibus edition is at $4.99 and earning a consistent three to one ROI. Every single day for two months and counting.

Don't get fixated on anything that anyone says you must do. You don't have to do anything you don't want to. I encourage you to test the boundaries of your own value. Stay within budget and remember what you're trying to accomplish with your sales.

- Make money now
- Bring on more readers while not losing money
- Use a loss leader to expose your work to even more readers
- Reward current readers

Calculating read-through/buy-through

These calculations are not easy, and they take a bit of wickering to come to a final number. Let's use a trilogy where each book is $4.99 for our first calculation.

Ten copies sold of Book 1 are worth $49.90, at 70% minus download fee of $0.10/copy yield $33.93.

Five copies of Book 2 (a 50% buy-through rate) are worth $16.97 (70% and $0.10 download fee per copy)

Four copies of Book 3 (an 80% buy-through rate from Book 2) are worth $13.57 (70% and $0.10 download fee per copy).

That's a total earning of $64.47. Which means that each of the ten copies you sell of Book 1 isn't worth $3.39 in royalties, it's worth $6.45 because of buy-through. This is what happens when you only advertise Book 1 but have a link to Book 2 at the end of Book 1, and a link to Book 3 at the end of Book 2. If the readers reach the end, you provide them with the opportunity for instant gratification. This is also why pre-orders are effective. Get the reader to buy it when they are stoked about your last story. No need to remind them. They get the book when it publishes. They might be disappointed if the book isn't available yet, but if they liked the story enough, they'll buy the next one and wait for it to go live. Pre-order sales at full-price are good sales. If you change the price of the first book to $0.99 if you get as high as a 50% read through rate, every ten copies of Book 1 earn you $3.50, plus $16.97, plus $13.57 equals $34.04. It's much easier to get ten copies into new hands at $0.99 than it is to get ten copies of a first in series to new readers at full price.

Even if you don't get a 50% buy-through to Book 2, in the numbers game, you'll win if you can move copies at $0.99, unless no one is continuing to Book 2, but that's a different issue.

There are so many moving parts in this thing called self-publishing, but you can easily manage them all. None of these calculations are earth shattering. None of these prices are bizarre. This is in-the-box awareness for better brand establishment and revenue generation. Knowing how your price drives that process is not too difficult.

Calculating buy-through rate is simple. If you sell ten of Book 1 and five of Book 2, it's a 50% read-through rate. After Book 3, you want to see a 90% buy-through rate. That means for every ten copies of Book 2 you sell, you should sell nine copies of Book 3.

$$\frac{\text{Copies Sold of Book 2}}{\text{Copies Sold of Book 1}} = \text{Buy-Through Rate}$$

And then keep calculating that for however many books you have in the series (multiplied by 100 to get a percent). Do the calculations one after another and you'll see a gentle downward trend. Even with a 90% read through, you're losing one reader out of every ten with each new book. Unless you climb towards 100%, you will reach a point where it makes no financial sense to continue a series. In one of mine, it was eighteen books. In another, it was four. You never know until you start doing the math, although you'll have a feeling.

When calculating read-through rate, you need to add a calculation.

$$\frac{\text{Total Pages Read Book 2/KENPC for Book 2}}{\text{Total Pages Read Book 1/KENPC for Book 1}} = \text{Read-Through Rate}$$

Then, when people mix and match, it makes your calculations problematic along with reading rates. Most people won't binge the book in one day, so you'll get multiples of people contributing to a whole calculation. In the end (after you have a month or quarter's worth of data), it all evens out, but in the beginning, it's nothing more than an educated guess.

Look at your bottom line. Is it continuing to improve? That's what you're looking for. Keep track of your expenses so you aren't spending more to make the same.

And when calculating your ROI, take the full read-through/buy-through into account. You're not just selling Book 1. You're selling the whole product line (series or books on your brand). That's why the insurance companies bundle your home, auto, and pet insurance. It's easier to sell ten books to one person...

CHAPTER FOUR

Managing Reader Expectations

- Strategic pricing
- One book
- Series pricing
- Box set/omnibus pricing
- Pricing to drive KU page reads
- Pricing based on author accolades
- Raising the price
- Varied pricing
- Step increase pricing

This chapter is the heart and soul of your pricing strategies. How can you get the most from your book by using pricing to help drive and sustain sales? How do you get your readership comfortable with your pricing structure?

The only way I know to accomplish all of this is through communication and precedent. If you need to change your precedent, you need to ratchet up your communication. I used to launch my books at $0.99 and leave them that way for a week to drive sales numbers. I have moved away from that, but the first time, there was a little friction with the readership.

When you change your prices, you'll get accused of being a money grubber. Expect it, unless you change them downward. You can run discounts all the time, but that will train your readers to buy your books for next to nothing, which means you get a percentage of next to nothing. Naught plus naught, let me see, carry the zero...

You can make more than that if you strategize how best to get readers into your books. And that is the foundation of your strategy. It starts with finding your readers.

1. Targeting the right readership with your marketing (you have to do that no matter what your price)
2. Set up your marketing campaign (decide your prices and get your ads & promotions in place)
3. Keep writing

The targeting is nothing more than finding the genre where the most readers who like your book will be hanging out. Your marketing campaign is to tickle their fancy. I write science fiction. This is a broad genre, but my stuff appeals across most of the subgenres, so I target science fiction. I don't do newsletter swaps with authors in other genres. I don't try to shoehorn my science fiction into a fantasy group. I advertise to readers of Sci-Fi.

Prices in my genre are $4.99 for regular price, $0.99 on sale and occasionally, bigger names will throw out a book for free, but it'll be the same one they've been giving away the past few years.

. . .

Strategic pricing

No price stands tall over the long term which means that you will most likely change prices whether regular price to a different regular price to a discount to free and back to the regular price.

The bigger the name you have and more popular you are with your readers, the easier you'll have it. Just make yourself a household name and advertising gets a whole lot easier from there. Then all you need to do is let them know you have a new book out. Letting them know is the entirety of your effort. Your book's price is what they pay because that's how you've trained them.

The rest of us have to have marketing plans. Mine is that I publish the book on Monday at $1.00 off full price and have it in KU. The book is at $3.99 for the first five days. For my superfans who buy it when it first comes out, they get a discount. For those with KU subscriptions, they get to read it. And then on Saturday (five days later), I drop the price to $0.99 for one day and call it fan pricing (this was originated by Mal Cooper and Michael Anderle has perfected the technique with discounts every Saturday that drive sales numbers nice and high to round out a week's worth of numbers). I get the week of downloads and some sales with a big rise in sales on the sixth day. That gets the rank and exposure look that Amazon seems to like to help carry the book at full price for the next seven days.

Amazon sends the emails to those who follow me sometime after that fifth day, unless I've done a pre-order then the follower email could go out sooner. Amazon doesn't share the number of followers that you have. I guess it's a decent number because I get a nice bump in sales when that email goes out. Getting followers on Amazon was easier when you could run giveaways, but that program ended on October 12th,

2019. I always have links in the back of my books asking people to follow me on Amazon. Even though I don't have any control over that list, I don't pay anything to maintain it or send emails to it. Amazon will send an email to my followers with each new release. I do nothing except release the book. They take care of everything else. And when it goes out, I pick up an extra 100 to 200 sales for a book that is at full price. Sometimes even more. It's another nice bump to stretch out the sales and keep the exposure at a place where Amazon may take notice and give it a little extra nudge.

If that book is the first in a series, it'll start going on sale and getting promotions when the third book hits the street. If it's the second or later book in the series, it won't go on sale again except as part of a box set after the single book sales have run their course.

That's my general strategy. But there are plenty of other strategies. Joe Solari put this chart together to highlight the volume of sales you need to have in order to realize the same margin as a single $4.99 sale.

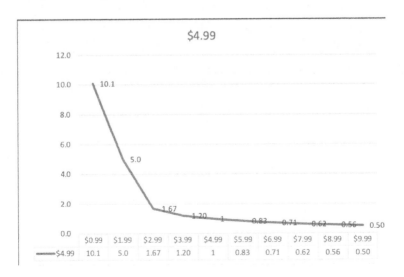

	$0.99	$1.99	$2.99	$3.99	$4.99	$5.99	$6.99	$7.99	$8.99	$9.99
$4.99	10.1	5.0	1.67	1.20	1	0.83	0.71	0.62	0.56	0.50

At $0.99, you need ten times the sales, five times at $1.99. Those are some eye-opening numbers if you are running random sales without a strategic purpose or an eye toward new readership.

One book

With one book, you need to make a profit off that one book, which means your marketing (and pricing) campaign should focus on regular price or a slight discount, but not a deep discount because you have to move too many copies to make money. This is the most significant challenge in the entirety of self-publishing: how to sell one book.

Dress for the job you want. Put a cover on your book that is genre appropriate and every bit as eye-catching as the top books in your genre. Remember: genre = marketing. No one cares about a ten-book mashup with a crossover. Does it have vampires? Now you're talking—hit the paranormal genre and keep going. Don't overthink it because you'll start losing readers.

What are single book prices in the paranormal genre? What about first in series? There should be a difference. Prices are from $2.99 to $14.99. The legacy publishers have books from $8.99 to $14.99 while the indies are sporting the lower prices. What if you published your book at $8.99? Make it look like one of those others. Killer blurb and a great story, then target your ads at your fellow vampire books. Genre = the biggest chunk of readers who may like your book. But my vampire doesn't do vampire things, he's more like a superhero. Fine, then go over to the Superhero genre and start your research. If you try to jump around genres because you're not sure, then you're going to spread yourself too thin and not find traction in either place. Find the biggest genre and go after it.

If that doesn't work, then find the next biggest. This isn't a book on marketing, but your marketing plan has to be based on genre, because genres are very different. Prices are different and the readers react differently.

Don't despair. Take off your artist hat, put on your business hat, and start researching. It's the internet. You'll go down a rabbit hole or two, but you wrote your book and you know what you like. What is the biggest genre that you like that is in your book? Pick that one. And stop waffling. Every book is in more than one category. That's why Amazon lets you have up to ten.

The bottom line: sell that one book at the highest price you can manage in order to maximize profitability from each and every sale. Find the price point where your book belongs and sell the hell out of it.

None of the above applies if you are using this book to gather email addresses or leverage some part of your brand for future sales. That's a different strategy where you are trying to maximize your profitability with read-through/buy-through. I talked about that above.

But for one book, my best advice is to write another book. With multiple books, your marketing life becomes a whole lot easier. With one book, you must become a master at advertising, whether Facebook, Instagram, in person, Amazon Advertising, because you need to sell people your full price book. Your competition will be from people who are selling discounted books.

Series pricing

You can sell the characters in a series or you can sell yourself (you are the brand). Right up front, series are the cat's ass when it comes to profitability. When readers care about the characters who have given them an emotional high, the readers will stay on board, wanting more of their favorites.

Give it to them. You've done the hard part of hooking them, now keep them on the line by feeding them more volumes. You don't need to write and publish a book a month. All you need to do is live up to the promises you made to your readers. If you promised two books a year, deliver two books a year. Build the trust. Many old school authors have been writing for forty years, but they've published two books a year every year, and their readers eat them up.

It also makes your advertising easier. You can discount Book 1 and use it as a loss leader. You don't need to make a profit on that one volume. All you need is to get people into the story, let them fall in love with the characters. There are multiple schools of thought regarding the first in a series. Discount it, price it low always, or sell it at a full price.

I have enough books that I do all of these.

Free first in series

Permafree is a discount. Cast it far and wide, but don't. What I mean here is that even though it's free, you need to manage reader expectations. "A full-length sample so you can see if you want to board the train with thousands of other happy fans..." and then quote your best reviews of the series. Free has value if you treat it as such. I personally dislike the word "freebie." It's not linked to anything. "Get your freebie today!" That does the author a disservice, in my opinion. Other wording links your book to a future where the potential reader is enjoying the rest of the series, but there's no risk to give it a try.

Again, targeting. Even a free book needs to be offered to the right readers.

Shape your Permafree message well. It's your ad copy which is every bit as important as your blurb. "Opening the door is free. Stepping inside comes at a cost." For my free books, I'll list the series at the end. Readers can look at the series page. They'll see if they want to keep reading, they have to pay for the pleasure. I also note in various places that I'm a professional author and can't afford to work for free, but I'm more than happy to offer that one sample because I want my readers to spend their money wisely on those things that are most important to them.

I do care. I don't want miserable people leaving me one-star reviews because I hornswoggled them and that includes the perception of hornswoggling. Because the perception of getting ripped off or lied to is enough to make someone upset. It's important to do everything you can to minimize misperception. That is what managing reader expectations is all about.

What about loading up the first three (or so) chapters on BookFunnel? If those words account for less than 10% of the book, then you won't run afoul of Amazon's KDP Select terms of service. If your book is wide, then there are no Amazon impacts. Make sure you have your disclaimer up front on those three chapters. "Here are the first three chapters of BEST BOOK EVER, but only the first three because I don't want you to waste your money buying a book that you won't like. You'll know after the first three chapters. I'm a professional author which means that I have to sell my books in order to put food on the table. When I have a few more books, I may offer this entire title for free, but right now, the best I can do is show you how the book starts so you can decide if the rest of the story is worth $4.99. I also love dogs."

You can never start early enough in building a relationship with your readers. I want to make them laugh while also having a serious side. And I don't want to give a book away if I don't have to. If they are reading that disclaimer, then they will be well aware of the reading risk. If they like it, it'll come with a future price tag of $4.99.

If you make the whole book free, you can still use targeted advertising, Newsletter swaps, promotions, and many other ways to get your book into the right reader's hands. Have you ever been to Vegas and walked along the street? There will be guys pressing prostitution business cards into every hand that passes. You'll see those cards all over the ground. Throwing your free book at everyone who walks by is just like that. Give it to readers of your genre. Give it to readers of the secondary genres. Keep finding those readers. You'll be surprised at how hard it is to give a book away. If I'm going to do all that work, I'm more likely to ask them to pay $0.99 for my troubles.

Discounted first in series

The cornerstone of marketing a series is the discounted first book. The appetizer comes at a lower price than the main course, even if it's the same size. Here's a great thing about readers. Every story they consume only makes them hungry for more with a bottomless pit for a stomach. If any author converts a TV-watcher to a reader, all authors win. No matter how slowly they read, there's a good chance they can read more books than we can write.

When do you discount your first in series and for how long?

I'll answer that question with "as long as you need to." Five to seven days once a quarter is usually good enough. That gives you time to run extra ads, make it rare enough to generate interest, and drop it across as many promotions as you can hit during that period.

For a single volume, $0.99 is an attractive price point in sales circulars. Even Freebooksy (who use the term "freebies" much to my chagrin) will have the $0.99 deal of the day at the bottom of their Freebooksy Newsletter which is built of readers looking for free samples of full-length books. The good thing that Freebooksy does is that they parse by genre. So even if your book is $0.99 and not free, the readers could be in your general genre. This works well for science fiction and goes back to targeting. Don't waste your efforts paying to put your book in front of readers who aren't your genre. You're paying for nothing.

If you are looking for a rank bump, then you'll need to stack promotions, that is run a variety of promotions over at least a five-day period. In order to make sure that your discount price is in effect, you should set it up to start at least one day prior and end a full day after. Also, an important safety tip is that the distributors who control the prices of your books (Amazon, B&N, Apple, and Kobo) have the best customer service during the work week. If you want to discount your book starting on Saturday, Sunday, or Monday, I suggest you do it on the Friday before so that if the price does not change, you can get the customer service A team and get it fixed before you are out any money on paid promotions, ads, or other marketing.

Making sure that your book is at the same price across all platforms is important. Google has been notorious for randomly discounting books and, out of the blue, Amazon matches; all of a sudden, your ROI tanks because your price is too low. Give your stuff a cursory glance at least daily. You want to control what is in your control and that includes pricing. You can get aberrant price changes fixed.

Once you've changed your price (if not doing a Countdown Deal or using Kobo's discount pricing tool) and confirmed that your new price is in effect, you start beating the bushes with your organic sources. You've done the hard work months prior when you set up your swaps and promotions. You didn't? Then you may not get as much out of your promotion as possible.

But don't despair if you don't have any money. There are sites that run free promotions, although they have limited targeting and you may not get a great response, but when you invest in your business, balance your time versus money. If you have no money, then you set up with every free promotion that will have you. As well as newsletter swaps and shares. You've built your list and carefully cultivated it with your readers. This doesn't have to cost you anything either, until you start getting bigger numbers (over 1,000 subscribers kind of numbers).

What if you only have one book, no subscribers, and no money? Remember where I said this wasn't easy? Invest your time. You need to write a story or use other methods to get subscribers on board so you can share when the time is right. I'm not going to blow smoke up anyone's backside. If the only thing you've done so far is write the book, congratulations! That puts you in the minority of people who said they were going to write a book. Now, take off your artist hat and put on your business hat. With your business hat on, you'll see yourself as a person with an idea. You now have to establish your entrepreneurial chops. You need to set up and run your business.

People with one book do not have a product line. They only have the potential of one. Get your book out there and start advertising, build some organic readers, and keep writing. In this case, please don't make your book free unless you're using it as a funnel for people to join your list. If you discount it, then run paid promotions to get more readers on board and put your newsletter sign up in both the front and back matter. With one book, you're building a brand. If you want to make money off one book, then don't discount it—find a different way to build the buzz.

Back to discounting the first in your series.

Make it easy for readers to find the other books in the series. Put that link to the next book immediately after the end of the story. Make it one-click easy and your sales department will thank you because that means they have to do less. I know. We're indies. "They" is you. You'll thank yourself for saving time and increasing sales. Because that's entirely what getting your book 1 into people's hands is all about.

Here's a Reedsy-published case study about a month long $0.99 marketing campaign that worked out well.

Natalie worked with two Reedsy editors to ready her manuscript for publishing: Katrina Diaz on a structural edit and Aja Pollock on a copy edit. She also hired a professional cover designer.

She decided to publish her novel exclusively on Amazon and put it on a 30-day price promotion for $0.99. During that time, she read up on Facebook Ads and David Gaughran's Let's Get Digital for marketing advice.

After gathering ten positive reader reviews on Amazon (the minimum threshold for many book promoters), Natalie scheduled a Kindle Countdown Deal ($0.99 for one week) and booked with as many book promoters as she could. At the same time, she created AMS ads which allow authors to advertise their book below the "Also Bought" section of other books. During her Kindle countdown deal, she started seeing significant sales (peaking at 200 sales in one day). Knowing her sales would dwindle when the promotion ended, she ensured she had AMS ads ready to run every day after her Kindle countdown deal, which allowed her to sustain a positive *ranking. It was at this point Thomas & Mercer reached out to her about signing her novel.*

Please note that Natalie's CD was scheduled in the time period allowed outside of her 30-day run at $0.99.

This review supports one of my efforts where I did not wrap Amazon Advertising around a sale promotion.

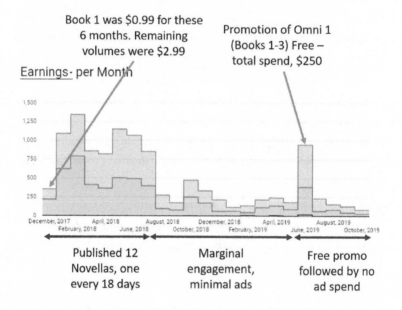

We had the one bump after spending some money on a number of promotions for our Free Omnibus.

Start your price planning three months prior to when you want to run your discounts. The first in series will earn you the read-throughs and buy-throughs you need to make money. As stated previously, there are only two reasons they don't work: You targeted the wrong audience, or there's a problem with the book. That's it.

Pushing a first book for thirty days at $0.99 can get one noticed. I would not follow Natalie's model because my priority is not to get a traditionally published book deal. I don't want to lose artistic control or donate a big chunk of my royalties, although if someone is going to pay you to increase your exposure, I'm good with that. I'd sign with 47North (an Amazon imprint, a traditional publishing model) for exposure to gain a broader outreach and engagement effort (which is everything else that I do).

If you have a permanently discounted first in series, then it might be a challenge to find new promotions but it's not impossible. Many highly successful authors maintain a prominent Permafree title (or three if they have plenty to choose from). Same with that permanent discount, but you won't be getting a BookBub featured deal unless you can discount your book at least 50%.

I'm a fan of periodic discounts and returning your book back to full price in between. I think it gives you more options. Unless you've published wide, then there are risks and efforts related to getting your books at the same price at the same time across all platforms. Those risks are even greater at Free because Amazon might not price match your other vendors. Whether you like them or not doesn't matter. They have 85% of the ebook market.

If you write nonfiction, let them fall in love with how you weave your narrative. You are your brand for a nonfiction series, but they don't sell-through as well as a fiction series because each topic may or may not resonate with readers. They will pick and choose based on what they want from the nonfiction titles, so discounting the first in a nonfiction series may not be as beneficial as keeping them all the same (regular) price and running your marketing campaigns based on your expertise in that subject. My nonfiction brand is based off my success with my fiction brand and non-profit work with 20Booksto50k®. What is your nonfiction niche? This is what you must go after when you figure out who those readers are who will like your work.

Full-price first in series

Marketing opportunities for this are limited to regular sales platforms (Google, Amazon Ads, Facebook Ads, and so on) and newsletter shares with other authors. I run my ads and spend a fair bit on campaigns for both Facebook Ads and Amazon Advertising. You must do something to tell people your series is out there. It also gives you the opportunity to discount the book to run more targeted promotions.

Are you counting on a different series to lead into a secondary series that is full price? I do that, too. Make sure your link taking readers to the next series is at the end of the last book, first thing they see after their favorite series wraps up. "Here's more of what you like!" is a powerful message.

As long as you are driving traffic that has been conditioned regarding full prices, you'll get what you need from that follow-on series. I've tried running it as a standalone series and it has done quite well in that regard. At the right side of this chart, I'm not advertising the follow-on series at all. That's pure profit.

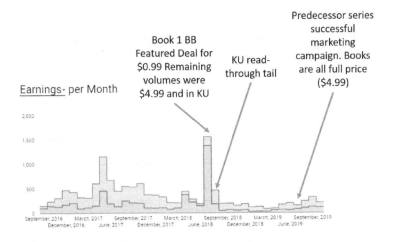

There is a place for a full-price first in series. Make it match the rest of the titles in your series and then discount and run promotions to keep the series earning money for you.

Other series pricing issues. I have one series where the books are wildly different in length, from 51k words to 117k words. I tried pricing them based on their length. Based on my reader feedback, you'd think I was torturing puppies. The perception is based off what the readers see as the lowest price. When I raised the price of the shorter volumes to match the price of the longer ones, the grousing stopped. Don't go through what I went through. Price every "book" the same in your series, even if they're novellas. On my series that I show above, I priced the first book (albeit, it was only 17k words) at $0.99. I received plenty of "input" that the whole series should have been that price.

No. I raised the price of the first in the series to $2.99. Maybe my readers are a little more price sensitive than other authors' readers, but damn. Manage your reader expectations. Tell them what the books cost.

. . .

Box set/omnibus pricing

This gets touchy based on the restrictions Amazon has in place for authors to participate in the KDP Select program. To get a 70% royalty rate, you must price your book between $2.99 and $9.99. If you write books that are earning $7.99/copy, bundling the trilogy means you have to charge $19.99 to earn the same as you could at $9.99. A bundled package in this case might only be $9.99 at 70% versus $15.99 at 35%. If you discount the bundle to $14.99 or even $13.99, you're the big loser when it comes to revenue. You can drive just as many sales, if not more, at $9.99 and you'll make more money as well as drive readers to borrow the bundle in KU earning the page reads which could surpass a single book's sale revenue.

I usually do three for the price of two, unless I go into the Amazon dead zone of higher than $9.99. I'll include three $4.99 books for $9.99, but I do have one box set of nine books that are $4.99 individually, yet the box is $9.99 regular price.

If the bundle exceeds $19.99, you're into making money again. Unless you're wide, then the bundles aren't reduced below 70% (60% effective if you use an aggregator like Draft2Digital) no matter the price.

Can you price your books higher on competing sites? Yes, but the other sites will match your lowest price. It's best to keep them all the same, except for Google Play and then you need to price it higher as they'll run random discounts that the other retailers will match. It all depends on how much of your revenue comes from Amazon. If it's 70% to 80%, you might be better off playing by their rules and pricing to $9.99 to earn 70%, but in that case, only bundle two books at a time. I've bundled up to nine and still priced at $9.99 because I believe my readers are more sensitive to high prices.

But I've priced all my box sets at $9.99, discounting them

for a month at a time to $4.99 (based on how a couple different omnibus editions drove page reads at that price). From there, I can discount a box set to $2.99 (I no longer go below that price, but it has taken me some time to get here) for promotions. At $0.99, I was getting a huge number of sales, few page reads, and no page read tail. People were simply buying the books. When I asked some of my readers why they didn't simply pick it up in KU, they were very complimentary, and it was nice for my ego. "I want these books anytime because they're so good."

And I lost my ass when it came to revenue. If they have to have it, they can at least pay $2.99 so I can get a $2.00 royalty. That's also a point at which they wonder if they want to pay it or not—these are my KU readers, about 60% of my revenue comes from the page reads. $4.99 was the tipping point that increased my page read tail. I also get sales at the regular price of $9.99, but not enough to increase revenue. It's revenue neutral (I sell fewer but make more with each sale). For a revenue-neutral effort, I'd rather put my books into more hands because they might buy books from one or more of my other series. Dedicated readers are worth more than a revenue-neutral price increase which can also have a positive long-term effect of increasing what the readers are willing to pay. I'll do it, eventually, but for now, I'm good at $9.99 discounted to $4.99 and occasionally down to $2.99 for promotions.

All of that and it's not the end all. I know authors in my genre who are killing it with page reads for box sets priced at $0.99. And they have them priced that way for months at a time. I personally buy their box sets for a buck rather than KU them, just because I do research all the time and switching around the ten titles I have in KU is annoying. I can see why my fans are buying my low-priced omnis instead of borrowing them. Maybe my targeting is too narrow? It's easier to borrow from an unknown author than buy, so maybe that's why they do so well. They also have aggressive marketing campaigns with newsletter shares, promotions, and advertising on multiple platforms. In the graph below, the red area indicates revenue from sales, and the blue area is revenue from page reads.

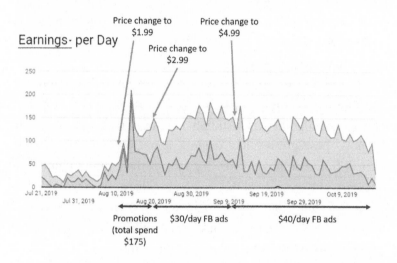

Back to the pricing strategies for box sets/omnibus editions. I like the hell out of $9.99 as a regular price but I am almost all-in with Amazon. If you are wide, all bets are off regarding pricing since you still get your 70% at $10.99 to whatever. Just be consistent. If you have multiple box sets for a single series, you can list them as their own series. My Darklanding series is a prime example of this. We have twelve books in the Darklanding series. We have four books in the series called Darklanding Omnis. For the omni editions, each volume is $5.99 (three $2.99 books for the price of two because these are all novellas). We also had audiobooks done for each omnibus volume to make them more attractive. I'll be running a major promotion soon, emphasizing all of that.

And we'll do a single bind-up of all twelve volumes, combining the audio into a single edition as well. The best thing about omnibus editions? It's almost no work to put one together, and it creates an entirely new revenue stream. These are FAR different from the book-stuffing scams that some of you may think of. These are different collections consolidated of the same books, but they are noted clearly in the titles and blurbs. You are not packaging the same five books five different ways. These are different collections, and they are all above board. If you are lost in regards to this conversation, then you have been insulated from the ridiculous people out there trying to steal from you. And it's okay because we've come through that and are able to repackage our own books to improve reader experience while allowing us to market to different audiences.

Do omnibus editions cannibalize sales of your individual books? No. There's a little overlap in readership, but you can find all-new readers with your omnibus editions, especially if the regular price is a discount from the individual book prices. On Amazon, the single books and omnibus editions are not linked in any way. A search for a book within the omni sometimes doesn't return a result of the omnibus edition. Bizarre but true, so advertising is the only way people will know these exist.

You can target the same general readers (genre specific, including your own list) As long as you keep running the usual quarterly or semi-annual promotions with your first in series, you may see a small drop-off in sales (beyond the usual drop when re-running the same book in the same paid promotion venue), but it's more than made up for with the added sales and page reads, if in KU, of the omnibus edition(s).

I don't create an omnibus edition until about a year after the books are out to make sure that the individual sales have run their course. BUT, an alternative that Michael Anderle has tried is to release the box set edition first, before releasing the three individual books—an omnibus for $4.99 made up of three individual books that will be $4.99 each. This strategy was based on the fact that we lose a greater percentage of readers between the first and second books than the second and third. Once the reader is into the third book, usually they stay on board, plus, all the marketing dollars go to selling the first book in the series. The added length of the three-book omnibus edition makes a KU payout offset the costs before getting into additional volumes in the series. The pricing in this case was $4.99 for the omnibus edition, which also drove the KU page reads and this was a multi-box set series (four omnis of three books each).

We have not broken out the individual books to publish them separately yet to determine if the reverse strategy pays dividends since we firmly believe there are two different markets, but did we cannibalize the individual book sales by releasing the omni edition first? A good question that we do not have the data for yet.

Pricing to drive KU page reads

Our data suggests you'll start seeing an increase in page reads up to 9 to 14 days after your promotion. I use BookReport to track sales using Amazon's data. The chart from BookReport will show an increasing separation between the pink sales and the blue page reads. While sales may flatline or decrease, your page reads should continue to increase. The omnibus graphic in the section above is a perfect example of how pricing can drive page reads, but also drive sales.

In some cases, the choice of $0.99 is enough for someone

to select to read it in KU. In other cases, you can list the book for Free and you'll get page reads because people click the promotional link and Amazon's default is "Read for Free" for KU subscribers. People click that instead of the less obvious "Buy for $0.00" link.

In experimenting, when pricing an omnibus edition at $9.99, I got fewer clicks than when priced at $4.99. It appeared that people had to consider the sale price to be a deal before reading it as part of their KU subscription. That's weird data, but I'm not sure it's an outlier. For single books, whatever your current readership delivers in a ratio of page reads to purchases is what you should expect when marketing a full-price single volume. For Facebook ads, I always start with "Kindle" as my primary group from which I refine the subsets. I want people who use the Amazon reading app or the Kindle devices themselves. I'm generally around two to one page reads to sales revenue, but that is slowly changing to 60/40.

Clear as mud? Test your prices and understand that it may take a week for the readers to start getting into your story and for the page reads to pick up. Patience and diligence will deliver the information you need to make better business decisions.

Pricing based on author accolades

Based on nothing firm, I believe that author accolades only deliver a marginal increase in exposure and no automatic entry into the higher pricing club. *The New York Times* Bestselling Authors and *USA Today* Bestsellers put that on their covers. BookBub includes it in their ads. Award winners put the award on the title—"A 2019 Award Winner." I've also seen "Million Selling," "Bestselling," and "International Bestselling Author." Bestselling and International Bestselling have only arbitrary definitions, although many authors are firm in their belief about how they are defined. It is a great way to start an author fight without earning any additional sales. I suggest you stay away from the arbitrary on your book covers.

Authors write for readers. Are readers swayed by such things? Less and less in the era of "everyone gets a trophy." I don't know what's real. I know personally that I am not influenced by such proclamations. I am a Dragon Award Finalist for the Best Military Science Fiction Novel of 2018. I am proud of that book. It was a good one, but the third in a series, so it didn't get the traction necessary to win. And it had the saddest ending of any story I've ever written. That killed my read-through to books four and beyond. That is what matters to me. I put the award nomination in the blurb for the book, but not on the cover. I haven't used it anywhere else except when applying for a BookBub Featured Deal.

In the days of legacy publishing, authors and publishers touted their places on the NY Times Bestseller list as a testament to the quality of the book (and the implication that everyone on the planet should buy it). BUT, thanks to William Peter Blatty (author of *The Exorcist*) in 1986, NY Times convinced the court that its list was editorial content only, not a reflection of sales numbers. He claimed that he lost $3,000,000 because his book *Legion* was not included. But that was 1986 when people subscribed to the NY Times print copy and there was no internet (not like today, it was BBS based for information sharing back then—yes, I've been online since 1986 when I started with my 1200 baud modem).

In 2019? How many people make their book-buying decisions based on the NY Times lists? For those at the very top, they've been pushed and marketed in a way that the legacy publishers already know about their titles. Amazon pushes its imprint titles (a new traditional publisher) to its tens of millions of book buyers. Amazon can sell books. It's what they do (along with a lot of other stuff as a testament to my credit card statement each month).

Can you price your stuff higher? Looking at circumstantial evidence, I don't see it. When you publish exclusively through Amazon, you won't hit USA Today or NY Times Bestselling author lists (and Amazon won't put that label on their imprint book titles even if the author hit the lists with books that aren't under their imprint) because those two lists require a certain number of sales from other distributors like B&N and Apple.

An example is Olivia Hawker's latest, *One for the Blackbird, One for the Crow* had "Bestselling Author of *Ragged Edge of Night*," her first title with Lake Union.

If you're interested, here is a list of the Amazon imprints as listed on the Reedsy blog.

- Amazon Publishing: general fiction and non-fiction, encompassing a number of genres
- Amazon Encore: publishes out-of-print works
- Amazon Crossing: publishes bestselling and award-winning books in translation in the United States
- Amazon Crossing Kids: a sister of Amazon Crossing, it specializes in translating children's books into English
- Amazon Original Stories: short fiction and non-fiction
- Lake Union Publishing: contemporary fiction, historical fiction, memoirs, and popular non-fiction
- Thomas & Mercer: mysteries, thrillers, and true crime novels
- Montlake Romance: romance
- Little A: literary fiction and non-fiction

- 47North: science fiction and fantasy
- Skyscape: teen and young adult
- Two Lions: children's books for readers up to 12 years old
- TOPPLE Books: spotlights the voices of woman of color, gender non-conforming, lesbian, bisexual, transgender, and queer writers
- Jet City Comics: comics and graphic novels
- Grand Harbor Press: self-help
- Waterfall Press: Christian fiction

The above is published with the permission of Reedsy (Ricardo Fayet) from their blog: https://blog.reedsy.com/amazon-publishing/

The jury is out whether putting accolades on your covers help you with the price. I don't know. I know that those who spend a great deal on marketing include it if they have it, but I think that has watered everything down to the point that readers no longer see it. I use the extra space on my covers for the artwork or eye-popping typography.

My conclusion is that I think the book or series must stand on its own in regards to price point. I think there's little if any influence from accolades, although the "million selling author" takes all the guesswork out of what the accolades mean. Two seven-figure authors I know are now including it on their books.

Include any accolades in your marketing, I'm not sure it makes a difference on your covers. I think the legacy publishers do it because they've always done it that way. Work smarter, not harder, and do things for a reason.

Non-US markets

The theories and principles I share in this book are sound for nearly any market. Some markets are significantly harder to tap than others.

- You have to research your target market prices for your specific genre
- Dress for the job you want; as in, make your book look like it belongs

I've had a hard time cracking certain markets, like India, Brazil, and Mexico. Even with a number of BookBub Featured Deals under my belt, I have still made almost no money from the Indian marketplace. Ads targeting Brazil get an awful lot of clicks and no sales. What is different in these places?

If I knew, I would change it. But the good news is that with Amazon, B&N, Apple, and Kobo, you can target the bigger markets—UK, US, Australia, Germany, Canada, and France. They are the bulk of online book sales—far and away, the majority of my sales come from the US and UK.

Consider the cost of your time. How much energy and time are you willing to put into cracking a market that may not pay off, even if you hit it big? I've been as low as #8 overall in the Canadian store. That's not a living wage. You hit that number in the US or UK store and your book is selling and you're making good money. Pricing strategies take advantage of market conditions by applying the maximum price readers in that market are willing to pay for a title in your genre.

In some markets, that's pennies on the US dollar. I personally go after the markets where the payback is greatest. That's a business decision based on my available time.

Also, keep in mind that many non-US markets don't have their own Amazon store. Don't panic when you look at your KDP report and see sales at 35% when you have 70% selected.

If someone buys your book from Egypt, then you'll get the 35% rate without a download fee. Accept this as almost free money, because how else would you make a sale to a reader in Egypt? I personally would not. Those are good sales. Focus on the markets you are targeting.

Raising the price

As discussed above, most readers see the lowest price and think all books should be priced there. They have no concept about overhead costs, royalties, or margins. Once you have enticed them to come on board, however you do that, they need to know that there are certain prices you have to charge. This is why I launch a book at a dollar off, take it to a dollar for a day, then make it full price. The same way, every time. If they miss the sale, they know that's on them and why I have to charge a regular price, leaving it at that.

Then there are times where you raise the prices on your complete catalogue. I did with a series that I had at various prices based on the lengths of each volume within. It was a nice thought, but don't be like me. Determine what price is best for your genre and use that for all your books in that series. If you discount book 1, make sure your readers know why, but if they've been on board for more than one book, they'll get it. It still doesn't hurt to let them know and ask for their help in spreading the word.

"Join a great series by picking up Book 1 at the bargain price of $0.99, this month only. Deal ends on October 31, 2019." And raise the price come November 1st. A typical sales technique is the deadline. It creates a sense of urgency. "Only two left at this price!"

The most important thing you can do is keep your readers informed. I let them know whenever I want to change prices by using a deadline and sticking to it and making sure they get a last chance to buy a book before the price goes up.

Because you're always trying to make a sale, without being obvious about it, of course. I do get a flurry of last second sales no matter what, from my list that should have already bought the book. Strange but true.

For those people who priced their books at $0.99 upon release for the week in order to get that good Amazon algorithm love, they donate a lot of money with the hope for future sales based on an impression that Amazon will boost their book. Sometimes that's the case, and other times, it's not. I see very few authors doing this nowadays, at least in my genre. It's far too expensive for too little gain. You might get a good author rank, but that doesn't put food on the table. That magical boost is something you can't control. What you can control is a book that readers will love based on their experience with your previous books. Sell them on buying this book, and you'll get all the love you need. Maybe think about a $2.99 release special...

Let's look at the business side of this. When you launch a new title, you expect a certain percentage of your readers will either buy it or borrow it. Let's do the math for a 60k word book that has 300 KENP with a 50/50 ratio of page reads to sales. The first week you have two thousand sales and a comparable number of borrows and a 100% read-through rate by two thousand fans, too. Let's do the math if the launch is at $0.99.

$0.35 x 2000 = $700.00

2,000 x 300 x $0.004 (a low estimate for the rate) = $2,400

Total revenue that first week on a $0.99 book is $3,100.00

What if you priced it low for your fans, only $2.99 vice the regular price of $4.99. "Just for you, good people!" If there's a $0.10 download fee, then it's an even $2/copy sold.

$2.00 \times 2,000 = \$4,000.00$

$2000 \times 300 \times \$0.004$ (a low estimate for the rate) $= \$2,400$

Total revenue that first week on a $2.99 book is $6,400.00

That is a significant difference. At $0.99, maybe the KU rate changes to less than 50/50 because they want the book permanently on their bookshelf. Then the $0.99 author loses even more money. I take the step of educating my readership as to how KU works and how much I get paid for a title that they borrow and read, even if they read fifty books in a month, because it's evened out across all readers.

In the above example, each full read is worth $1.20. If a $2.99 price tag drives KU readers to borrow it instead of buy it, you still get over three times the revenue compared to a $0.99 sale. If they are on your list and have read and liked your other books, they are more than likely to read your newest book. Give them a reason to do the right thing by you, as a professional author who needs the revenue from each and every book. Those pennies add up over time. Before you know it, you'll be a six-figure author.

Set a price you can live with at the outset. Don't undersell and don't oversell. Too many people think their work is a masterpiece and they are crushed when the readers aren't smitten. Put on your business hat, price it just like the other books in that genre, and get to work figuring out how to sell your book to those readers.

There is plenty of information to help you do that, whether with Amazon, Facebook, BookBub ads, Twitter, Instagram, in person, or any other way you can imagine. It's only limited by your imagination and budget.

Just get the price reasonably close at the outset, the beginning of your career before you have a tidal wave of followers.

CHAPTER FIVE

Other Revenue Streams

- Paperbacks
- Hardbacks
- Audio
- Patreon
- Swag

The most important thing to keep in mind is that readers will spend their money on what is important to them. By giving them options, you aren't bilking anyone. You offer something and they buy it or they don't. How they spend their money is their decision. You need to be comfortable with that as part of offering other products for them to buy.

I have all my books made into paperback. I have many made into limited run hardbacks (for my dad, brother, and son). And I have a Patreon setup for those who want to be on the inside, see how the gears turn and maybe even influence the process a little bit. In the end, they may buy the book when it publishes, too. There's a lot to be said for giving your readers skin in the game. It turns fans into superfans and superfans are the ones who cosplay your characters and know more about them than you do.

I know you wrote the characters, but you'll have to trust me on this. Superfans will study your characters and draw conclusions and build profiles. Everyone wants superfans. They'll buy anything you have to offer, like that limited-edition hardback.

Paperbacks

Amazon makes the upload process easy for a paperback when you've published the ebook first. Many of the details carry over, like blurb and keywords.

Sometimes there are sizing issues with the new paperback. Once you get those resolved, use that file as your future template, and it'll be right the first time for your next upload. Cover artists have learned what they need to get the style and dimensions correct, so that also is now relatively painless (it was different with CreateSpace and that created numerous challenges when Amazon absorbed the titles and dismantled the CreateSpace interface).

But we're here to talk about pricing. At two different points during the upload process, you get the actual print-on-demand (POD) cost. When you upload the interior and cover files, you have to preview them. On that screen, you'll get the cost of printing, the royalty rates, and your profit (the bottom line). You'll also see it again on the pricing page. This is the price that Amazon customers in serviced marketplaces will see for a paperback. If the customer is in Amazon Prime, they'll get free shipping on your book. Your profit remains the same whether the customer pays for shipping or gets it included with their Prime membership. Don't sweat any of that—it is irrelevant to you. You see exactly what you'll get paid for a sale of your book. If you choose Expanded Distribution, then the data takes a slight turn.

With Expanded Distribution, the numbers change (not in your favor), and to make the same profit, you'll need to price your book higher. When you select the Other Marketplaces button, the pricing interface carries over your pricing. I manually change the prices to $0.99, but with the different country Value-Added Tax (VAT), your final price could look woefully different. You have to play with the prices to get the xx.99 look.

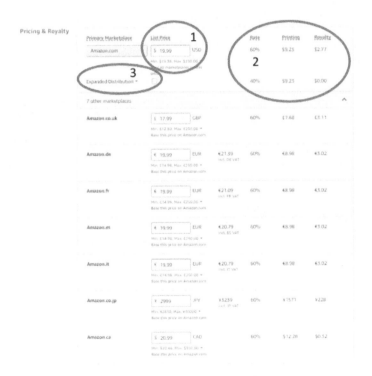

The screen above is from the KDP Print pricing page,

accessed via your KDP dashboard. In number 1, you can see what the minimum price must be. In this case, it's $15.38. If you look at the right side (number 2), Amazon breaks it out into clear terms. The cost of printing (this book is a beast at 720 pages), your royalty rate, and your profit for each sale. The calculations are simple. The price is $19.99, so 60% of that gives you $12, minus the production cost of $9.23 and you're left with $2.77 which is the number at the far right. If you change your price, your profit changes. You can play with the numbers to get them where you want. I usually like a profit of about $5/paperback. But this one was so big, I let it stand at $19.99 rather than make it $22.99, but also look at the other marketplace prices—they only look like they're $xx.99. See how the final price with VAT looks hokey? You have to play with the numbers. Here's what that looks like.

Marketplace	Price		Incl. VAT	Royalty	Cost	Profit
Amazon.co.uk	£ 17.99	GBP		60%	£7.68	£3.11
	Min. £12.80, Max. £250.00 ▾ Base this price on Amazon.com					
Amazon.de	€ 20.55	EUR	€21.99 incl. DE VAT	60%	€8.98	€3.35
	Min. €14.96, Max. €250.00 ▾ Base this price on Amazon.com					
Amazon.fr	€ 19.90	EUR	€20.99 incl. FR VAT	60%	€8.98	€2.96
	Min. €14.96, Max. €250.00 ▾ Base this price on Amazon.com					
Amazon.es	€ 20.18	EUR	€20.99 incl. ES VAT	60%	€8.98	€3.13
	Min. €14.96, Max. €250.00 ▾ Base this price on Amazon.com					
Amazon.it	€ 20.18	EUR	€20.99 incl. IT VAT	60%	€8.98	€3.13
	Min. €14.96, Max. €250.00 ▾ Base this price on Amazon.com					
Amazon.co.jp	¥ 3055	JPY	¥3299 incl. JP VAT	60%	¥1571	¥262
	Min. ¥2618, Max. ¥30000 ▾ Base this price on Amazon.com					

This is what happens when I check the expanded distribution box. The list price, as in, the minimum price I have to charge goes up $5 to make a profit of $0.77 for books sold through the expanded channels (like to libraries) but leave me with a profit of $5.77 for the Amazon direct-to-customer channels.

Pricing & Royalty

Primary Marketplace	List Price		Rate	Printing	Royalty
Amazon.com ⌄	$ 24.99	USD	60%	$9.23	$5.77
	Min. $23.07, Max. $250.00 ▾ Base all marketplaces on this price				
Expanded Distribution ▾	☑		40%	$9.23	$0.77
7 other marketplaces					⌄

What is Expanded Distribution? The following explanation is directly from Amazon.

Booksellers and libraries purchase paperbacks from large distributors. If you enroll your paperback in Expanded Distribution, we'll make your book available to distributors so booksellers and libraries can find your book and order it.

We currently work with US distributors, but booksellers and libraries outside of the US may purchase books from these US distributors. It's free to enroll your paperback in Expanded Distribution, and it allows your book to be made broadly available outside of Amazon.

Enrolling your paperback in Expanded Distribution doesn't guarantee it will be ordered by a particular bookseller or library. The decision to order your book lies solely with the individual booksellers and libraries. We can't provide details on which booksellers and libraries purchased your book.

If you make a sale through Expanded Distribution, you won't find out to whom. I don't select Expanded Distribution, but I know people who sell good quantities of books through the program. I believe it depends on genre and that nonfiction or any of the genres that have a good footing across multiple platforms outside of Amazon have more success with this.

These restrictions are a holdover from legacy publishing. I suspect they will eventually go away, just like personal ISBNs. I don't think those will be as important in the future as they were five years ago. This is also a holdover for an aging logistics train. Change is the only constant, so these things will change, and we'll have to flex accordingly. Indies will be able to adjust quicker than the legacy publishing houses.

Ingram—Lightning Source and Ingram Spark

Ingram's Lightning Source is a step up from Ingram Spark. Lightning Source requires an annual fee and is geared toward publishers and indies who move higher quantities of books. Spark is for indies but is still based on a legacy publishing model with steep discounts and returns possible (if you check those boxes).

Here's how Ingram Spark works. You upload your book and get a cost and minimum price point. They have a calculator to show you the numbers. From there, you price up until you get the profit margin you're looking for and then you can select a discount for distributors (10% to 15%) or wholesalers (40%) who might be interested in moving your books. You can discount up to 55% if you want, but you'll have to overprice your book or make no money, probably both if you select that option. You don't have to select any discount if your only target is to get your books into libraries. You don't have to enable returns in that case, either.

If you want your books in the usual brick and mortar store (Barnes & Noble), they generally won't buy your book unless they can return them. I've heard that the current returns are upwards of 30% from B&N. Other stores aren't returning books at anywhere near that rate even though many won't touch a paperback unless they can return it.

Standard pricing in IS applies. You'll have to research titles comparable in genre and length as your book and then see what kind of cost you get. For a 70k-word Western, the paperback retails for $14.99. A 40% wholesale discount puts the book at $8.99 which leaves a margin of a little over $1. Not too different from Amazon Print.

Here's the rub. Amazon is Ingram's largest client.

But Ingram Spark does Expanded Distribution so much better! If you check Expanded from Amazon, they send it through Ingram's channels. That's why you can't use your same ISBN for Amazon and for your separate account at Ingram. If you want to use the same ISBN, then you cannot check the Expanded Distribution box with Amazon. It's like publishing directly with Apple Books, but also going through Draft2Digital. You confuse the system and create a black hole that swallows the universe.

Don't create a black hole that swallows the universe. You only get to do one Expanded Distribution, either through checking the Amazon box (and then they send it through Ingram) or you do it directly through Ingram.

Ingram charges fees. If you need to update your manuscript, there's a fee for that unless you have a coupon that you can get from various organizations where you're a member. They don't want you to change your book as much as you don't want to, and they're in a position to penalize you. I usually end up changing my print book's interior a good three or four times as readers find those recalcitrant typos.

How steep do you want to discount? Some authors have gone all the way to 55%, but with costs, discovered too late they were making pennies on the dollar. If I sold hundreds of copies, I would expect a bigger check than something that would cover a cheap lunch. Watch the numbers on Ingram's calculator and adjust your prices until you're comfortable with the profit margin you need to make it worth your while.

Hardbacks

You can get hardbacks through Ingram or through specialty stores. For pricing, it all depends on what you can get them for. That 70k-word Western? The author copy price for the hardback (embossed title on a cloth cover) was $10.99/copy with no minimum. Hardbacks at $19.99 to sell at a show or anywhere else in person.

That's right in there with the legacy publishing crowd. And next year, Ingram is going to roll out full color vinyl covers for the hardbacks, reminiscent of a textbook.

I've had hardbacks done through a specialty shop. These were bind-ups where we included a number of books under one cover for multiple series. I bought them with full-color interiors, glossy, magazine-style pages in 8 ½" x 11" with buckram covers. They were worth every cent because I only bought five copies of each—one for my dad, brother, son, and me with one left over. I have the extras and may use them in a mass raffle for my fans or I may sell the set at a ridiculous price. The sky is the limit. This is a rare item. Only one that will be signed by the author. It doesn't get any better than that.

Michael Sullivan, a multiple NY Times and million-selling author (using accolades to show that he knows what he's doing) bought a pallet of hardbacks and ran a Kickstarter to get his fans to buy the books. That went very well, and he sold his whole stock. For pricing, since he bought in bulk, the only variable was shipping. He was counting on selling 100% of the copies.

If you buy in bulk, you can get hardbacks at a much cheaper rate than print-on-demand. You might be able to get a couple thousand copies at a few dollars a copy. Make sure you've caught all the typos, because it'll be expensive to make changes after they've been printed.

And you'll have to manually and personally ship each one unless you're able to do drop shipping of some sort—that's where someone else handles the product for you, and it'll come at a cost. You'll need to work that into your pricing.

Audio

The greatest area of growth in the industry is in audio. How does an indie get in on that pricing? There's the rub. If you're with Audible, you have no control over prices. I paid narrators up front, so I own all my books listed on Audible, but as such, I'm the one responsible for selling them. I'm doing a crap job at it, but I get to keep 100% of my royalties and I earn fairly consistently. It'll take more than a year for each book to earn out (some longer than others), but owning it is a huge benefit, despite a big hit to the cash flow by paying the narrators. In a couple years, I'll be on the right end of the audio cash flow.

Findaway Voices is like the Draft2Digital of audiobooks. They can get your audios into the wider marketplace and, most important, into libraries where borrows earn you money. Get your audio into libraries. It is one of the most lucrative markets right now. Audible doesn't do that.

I also have audiobooks with Podium, Dreamscape, and Tantor. I received advances so, once again, I have no control over pricing. The best thing I've found to do with audiobooks is to network. There are folks out there who are extremely successful with audiobooks. Leverage your strength to help others and they may be the missing link to crack the audiobook market.

. . .

Patreon

Patreon is fairly new to indies. It's a monthly subscription service where you, as the author provide something unique for your Patreon subscribers. They pay you at the beginning of each month. During the month, you deliver your guaranteed items, whatever those may be.

For me, I set mine up to deliver a new chapter every week. New covers and artwork a full week before I share on Facebook, and unedited copies of my latest book (at a higher rate) before it is released.

Exclusivity is what makes people pay more. Access to their favorite author? What is that worth?

For me, it's $5/month for a chapter a week. It's $10 if you want to see more in progress work and provide input. $20/month if you want to be more intimately involved with the story (select a city name and describe the city) and get full credit in my author notes.

Since I publish a new book once every two months (or more), there's plenty of opportunity for people to be involved. And I can still split time with my Facebook followers who have no guarantees that I'll give their input any weight.

Patreon is only limited by your imagination. What other things are you willing to give? Maybe a picture of fans with your books on your website? But you gave the fans those books... "Gave" being relative since they're paying you a subscription fee. Maybe you send them a new signed paperback every month. I have about a hundred different books in my garage and I generally paid less than $5/copy. If a subscriber paid $20/month? Well worth a signed book and media mail shipping. You can't knock a profit margin over 100%.

And if you can satisfy your subscribers with only digital content... A chapter a week and you send them two bonus chapters, all unedited of work in progress. That's free money because you're doing the work anyway. You are writing the book. They may provide input that helps you write a better book. It's your choice whether you accept what they provide.

Give Patreon a whirl. It's free to sign up. Set your support levels carefully. Don't give away your artistic control. You're better off without that $10 than naming a character something that makes you cringe. Go away, think about your support levels, make sure you can meet your commitments, and then revise them. Underpromise and overdeliver. That will endear you to your subscribers.

Kickstarter (and other crowdfunding)

Kickstarter is a way for people to support you. Crowdfunding puts money into the creative bank before you deliver. If you don't meet your designated funding level, no one gets charged. It's a great way to gauge interest in your project, as well as honing your copywriting skills (ad copy), because you'll need to promise a future delivery of this wonderful thing called a book (and the audio and paperback, as well, at different funding levels). You'll need to price it to cover the fees along with the expenses—editing, cover, formatting, and maybe a few ads. If you set your funding level at $1,000, you'll get about $800 after Kickstarter takes their cut. If you've promised paperbacks, then the cost of printing them will have to come from your funds, although shipping can be an add-on (best to collect them separately because shipping costs range far and wide).

I've seen extremely successful people use Kickstarter to nicely fund their projects. I've also seen folks fail miserably. If you've never written a book and you're trying to get people to fund your efforts, you may not find a willing audience. I saw one individual attempt to buy a year abroad to research and write the next masterpiece. It didn't get funded, needless to say, because the person had no history of writing a full book, let alone a masterpiece.

Kickstarted programs are tough to fund if you don't already have followers, but they do teach you about marketing. You have to put your campaign in front of strangers and convince them to invest. If that doesn't teach you good marketing, nothing will.

Affiliate income

Through Amazon's affiliate program (affiliate-program.amazon.com), as well as anyone else who offers affiliate participation, you get a small percentage from each sale that your link generated. I use affiliate links on my website and drive a significant amount of traffic to the Amazon site. It doesn't take much after people have bought my book and I get affiliate credit for all those sales. An extra $200 or $300 a month? It's nothing to sneeze at. Remember, increasing your number of revenue streams is a good thing as it evens out the highs and lows of your monthly income.

For Amazon's program, take care you don't run afoul of their terms of service. You can use your affiliate link on Facebook, but not in a Facebook ad. You can't use your affiliate link in a newsletter, but if you send someone a direct email with a link, that link could be an affiliate link. You are also supposed to maintain a notice that you are using an affiliate link. Here's what Amazon has to say about that.

Hello Associate,

. . .

This is a reminder of your disclosure obligations under the Operating Agreement. Any time you share an affiliate link, it's important to disclose that to your audience. They will trust you more if you are transparent about where you are directing them and why. To meet the Associate Program's requirements, you must (1) include a legally compliant disclosure with your links and (2) identify yourself on your Site as an Amazon Associate with the language required by the Operating Agreement.

To comply with Federal Trade Commission (FTC) regulations, your link-level disclosure must be:

1. Clear. A clear disclosure could be as simple as "(paid link)", "#ad" or "#CommissionsEarned".
2. Conspicuous. It should be placed near any affiliate link or product review in a location that customers will notice easily. They shouldn't have to hunt for it.

In addition, the Operating Agreement requires that the following statement clearly and conspicuously appears on your Site: "As an Amazon Associate I earn from qualifying purchases." For social media user-generated content, this statement must be associated with your account.

Associates should also consider the relevant social media platform's guidelines. For example, Associates may use Facebook's Branded Content tool.

To read more about the FTC Endorsement Guides, visit: https://www.ftc.gov/tips-advice/business-

center/guidance/ftcs-endorsement-guides-what-people-are-asking#affiliate.

Don't worry about the scare tactics. Just follow the guidelines and you'll be fine. If you can use an affiliate link, why wouldn't you? It can defray the cost of your download fee. The cost of getting an affiliate link? Zero. Nothing but your time.

Swag

What is your strategy with your swag (the logo products that represent your brand)? Is it to reward your fans? If that's the case, you'll want to give the stuff away for free. If you bought expensive giveaways, then maybe you raffle them or reward them for special reason. Maybe you want your fans to buy branded merchandise only available from you. Merchandise isn't going to be high margin. It's superfan stuff. It may not hurt to have something.

I have some of my book stuff on Society6, where I own 100% of the covers (live models from a photoshoot with a purchased 3D ship in the background and all custom work under contract—no stock images without the proper extended licenses). I can put that on as much merchandise as I want. It's there, and I don't have to manage anything.

Fans can order it, or I can run a raffle and then I'll order, but Society6 will print and ship it directly to the fan. I stay out of that business because it's time consuming, but the swag is available. Like audiobooks, you have no control over the pricing from Society6, but you can let your fans know when they are running a sale (it used to be every Sunday). There are many more companies than just Society6 who do this. Find the one that's right for you and make sure you only use artwork that is within your legal rights to use.

Many authors make bookmarks. They are easy to print and inexpensive. You can put information on there to help guide readers or potential readers that you've met in person to your website or landing page. They can start their journey to becoming a superfan, but these are more promotional and have nothing to do with a pricing strategy. But they have everything to do with a branding strategy. What is your brand?

Embrace it and market it (just a little). Selling stuff is different than selling books. I much prefer selling my stories because everyone should love my characters as much as I do! "Let's talk about my main character..."

Have those conversations with your fans. It's amazing what you'll hear. Listen well, and you'll have fans for life.

CHAPTER SIX

In Closing

The earlier you decide your pricing strategies, the better off you'll be. First and foremost, focus on writing your book. Do that well; otherwise, all the rest is just throwing good money after bad. That said, your first book doesn't have to be "good," it simply has to be. It gives you a place from which you will measure your improvement. Accept that you are not going to write the perfect book. There is no such thing. Some books appeal to broader audiences, some to narrower audiences. No book appeals to everyone. Write the book and then write a better book. Is writing a part of your soul? That's a perfect thing there. There will always be another book. Now that you've written your first book (or more), you might as well make some money.

Before you publish that first book, the one thing you should have is a way to engage with your fans. We all start with none and end up with some. You need to hook them and keep them on the line. The easiest way to do that is with a newsletter. Set up your newsletter and put links to it in the front and back of your book. Give your future fans a way to find you.

A landing page might also help because it gives your potential fans a place to find all things that are you. The swag. The snippets from your life. A blog. Your book signings. Your movies. Your glamorous black-tie, red carpet... hang on. If that stuff is your goal, you better get to work. If you're like me, all you want to do is sell more books today than yesterday, more this year than last year. Over time, you'll find yourself in a good place. It helps to look back every now and then to see where you started and how far you've come.

We all started with nothing, no books, no author credit. Until we wrote that first book.

I've scattered one-liners throughout this book to help you focus on the goal of making more money over the long term.

- Dress for the job you want
- Act like you belong there
- The Godiva Chocolate Model
- Don't leave money on the table
- A long-term marketing strategy includes full price, discounts, and possibly books for Free
- It's easier to sell ten books to one person, than sell to ten new readers
- Box sets can be like free money
- Genre = Marketing
- Research your target genre and see what the prices are

Pricing is something you can set and forget, but it can cost you if you don't have what the market will bear. I lost a great deal of money with a box set at $1.99 when it sold equally well at $2.99. For that extra dollar in price, I would have pocketed an additional $1.25. How many copies did I sell? Enough that I cost myself a healthy chunk of a month's mortgage.

I now price my box sets at $9.99 and put them on sale for $2.99, and that's the lowest I'll go. I want to get the KU page reads, but I can make money off a sale at that point. I will raise the price on all my individual titles to $5.99 in 2020. I'll continue to advertise the first in series at full price and discount that very same first one every six to twelve months to $0.99 and hit the promotions hard. My real profit lies in the books that follow in the series as well as all my other series when I gain superfans.

If you only have a few books, you can do perfectly fine, but you have to invest more time and talent into marketing. You can't make a lifetime's earnings off a single book. That is a lot of money. Maybe someone has done that, but it's so far out of the norm, you might as well try to win the lottery—your odds are about the same. For the rest of us, and for those authors who are doing well, we are writing that next book, whether it takes a week or a year, we know that adding to our backlists is healthy for long-term prosperity.

The timing of your promotions depends on your strategic goals. If you have one book, you'll need to maximize profitability through full price or reduced discounts (a dollar off, for example). If you have a series of three books, then you have much more latitude with the first book. Free, $0.99, or a combination at regular intervals throughout the year to catch the largest number of readers from your genre. Your goal is for them to read your book. I'd give anyone a copy of the first book in a series if I had a guarantee they'd read it. I'm confident that science fiction readers will like my books. Having sold hundreds of thousands of books and earning thousands of five-star reviews, it's not just my ego. With my business hat on, I see marketable products with a track record of success.

If you don't have that track record, understand that I didn't either, not that long ago. It starts with the first good review from a stranger, as well as a low review highlighting real errors you can fix. Reinforce the good, fix the bad, and move forward.

Always keep moving forward and feel better about yourself with each new word. You are in control of the flow and impact. You determine the plot that keeps your readers engaged. And you make the magic happen, from within that wondrous place of your own mind through your fingertips or spoken words, into the computer, ultimately ending with a reader, a listener, a fan.

What is the value of your brand? Don't get wrapped around making a book Free. That's good marketing when targeting a readership that will come on board and buy the rest of your books. That's what that first Free book is worth, the retail price of the rest of your backlist.

It has a great value. And so do you. Don't price your books so low that you can't make ends meet. Don't price them too high where you aren't making any sales. Price them just right, for your market, your genre, and for you.

There is a sweet spot and, when you find it, your good books will breathe joy into your life. Pricing as part of a long-term marketing strategy plays a significant role in your future author health.

Thank you for reading this book. I sincerely hope that it has provided a way forward for you.

BIBLIOGRAPHY

These are the authors and books I mention in this book. Stop by and give their quality offerings a look. Check out their Amazon author page to see what else they have in their bag of supporting tricks.

Joe Solari
Business Owner's Compendium: A practical guide to the theory of starting, owning and operating a business
https://www.amazon.com/dp/B0728G3T7N
Joe's Author Page
https://www.amazon.com/Joe-Solari/e/B01MZ4KOPM/

Tammi Labrecque
Newsletter Ninja: How to Become an Author Mailing List Expert, @2018
https://www.amazon.com/dp/B07C6J8HP9
Tammi's Author Page
https://www.amazon.com/Tammi-Labrecque/e/B00Q7RSPEI/

Brian Meeks
Mastering Amazon Ads, @2017
https://www.amazon.com/dp/B072SNXYMY
Mastering Amazon Descriptions, @2019
https://www.amazon.com/dp/B07NSH2QLM
Brian's Amazon Ads working group on Facebook (learn more
about testing and running ads, to include ad copy) https://
www.facebook.com/groups/407283052948198/
Brian's Author Page on Amazon
https://www.amazon.com/Brian-D.-Meeks/e/B0073XZH78/

David Gaughran
Let's Get Digital: How to Self-Publish and Why You Should,
@2018 https://www.amazon.com/dp/B078ZNWD61
From Strangers to Superfans, @2018 https://www.a-
mazon.com/dp/B0798PH9QT
BookBub Ads, @2019
https://www.amazon.com/dp/B07P57V38D
David's Author Page on Amazon
https://www.amazon.com/David-
Gaughran/e/B004YWUS6Q/

Mal Cooper (look for all Mal's nonfiction books)
Help! My Facebook Ads Suck, @2018
https://www.amazon.com/dp/B078NBW3M3
Mal Cooper's Author Page
https://www.amazon.com/Michael-Cooper/e/B071FJHK9K/

Chris Fox
Relaunch Your Novel, @2017
https://www.amazon.com/dp/B071HVZD1G
Chris's Author Page

https://www.amazon.com/Chris-Fox/e/B00OXCKD2G

Bryan Cohen
How to Write a Sizzling Synopsis, @2016
https://www.amazon.com/dp/B01HYBWOF6
Bryan's Author Page
https://www.amazon.com/Bryan-Cohen/e/
B004I9WJTY/ref=dp_byline_cont_eBooks_1

Dave Chesson, Kindlepreneur
Book Marketing 101 & Publisher Rocket
https://publisherrocket.com/
Amazon Book Description Generator Tool
https://kindlepreneur.com/amazon-book-description-generator/

Mark Dawson
Learn Amazon Ads
https://www.amazon.com/dp/B06Y6BSRLR
Mark's Author Page
https://www.amazon.com/Mark-Dawson/e/B0034Q9BO8/
ref=sr_tc_2_0?qid=1521462397&sr=1-2-ent
Mark's outstanding Self-Publishing Formula course -
https://selfpublishingformula.com/

ACRONYMS AND TERMS

ACX—Audiobooks on Amazon

BB—BookBub (the gold standard paid newsletter promotion service)

ENT—eReader News Today (a paid newsletter promotion service)

KDP—Kindle Direct Publishing

KENP—Kindle Edition Normalized Page (count)

KU—Kindle Unlimited

ML—Mailing List

NL—Newsletter

POSTSCRIPT

If you liked this book, please give it a little love and leave a review. My wheelhouse is Science Fiction, but I have enough experience so the nonfiction makes sense and, hopefully, helps you out. If you like this, join the 20Booksto50k® Facebook group, as that's where all these conversations and explanations take place. Michael Anderle and I even have a few videos on a wide variety of self-publishing topics. So, you don't need to join my newsletter as I'm not going to promote nonfiction there. But if you like Science Fiction...

You can join my mailing list by dropping by my website www.craigmartelle.com or if you have any comments, shoot me a note at craig@craigmartelle.com. I am always happy to hear from people who've read my work. I try to answer every email I receive.

You can also follow me on the various social media pages that I frequent.

Amazon—www.amazon.com/author/craigmartelle
Facebook—www.faceBook.com/authorcraigmartelle
My web page—www.craigmartelle.com

AUTHOR NOTES

I am the blue-collar author. I have a law degree, but that doesn't matter, not when it comes to writing. What matters is the willingness to work hard at this thing called self-publishing. I've worked harder, not smarter, on a number of things. I've been fairly successful, but I have much more to learn. In this volume, I'm trying to offer a lot of that experience regarding pricing because there are no other books on the market specifically for author book pricing. Generic pricing models don't necessarily apply to the self-publishing industry.

Part of what helps me learn is helping others. That's what this book is all about. I am sharing what I've done, and I've made many mistakes, some more costly than others. I want to help you avoid those mistakes while also telling you that you aren't alone.

The biggest thank you of all goes to my friend, Michael Anderle. The business side of stuff is just a footnote to our conversations on life. We've made a difference in people's lives, helped them to help themselves. Taught them to fish, as it may be. It's a great feeling we share. Working with the hundreds of books published by Michael's company has given me insight into a variety of different approaches. We've tested nearly all of them.

Shout out to Joe Solari who provided a couple charts and additional business insight. We had a great conversation about Pricing Strategies, and that conversation is on YouTube somewhere.

The 20Booksto50k® Facebook group is, bar none, the best self-published author group in the world (in my muchly biased opinion). We are a not-for-profit group that exists solely to help others, share our successes, learn from our failures, and buoy each other's spirits. It's the place where drama comes to die. As indie authors, we work alone. Sometimes we're insulated from a lot of the real world, and I use that term loosely. So much that you read online is no longer real. It doesn't apply to you, or it's been sensationalized to the point that its only purpose is to get an emotional response. We keep that garbage out of the group and focus on what it takes to sell more books (ethically, of course).

We're proud of that group, and I get the pleasure of learning something new every day. Surround yourself with quality people and that's what you'll become.

A realistic attitude and hard-work is what wins at life. Not everyone has a breakout winner. I don't, but I keep telling better and better stories. I know the big one is coming. I'll keep working toward it and will price it right. :)

And there's no reason you can't have a big winner too. Work hard at the right things and make sure you earn your just desserts. Don't undervalue or overvalue your books.

Shout out to the review crew! What a great bunch of people.

- Fatima Al

- Lasairiona McMaster
- Joe Solari
- Erika Everest

Thank you all. You helped make this book better through your valuable input. The indies who pick up this volume will benefit. I hope we've answered most, if not all, of your questions. Write and publish. Take your business seriously and consider pricing as part of your overall marketing strategy.

There's never been a better time to be a self-published author.

Peace, fellow humans.

Craig Martelle

ALSO BY CRAIG MARTELLE

Terry Henry Walton Chronicles (co-written with Michael Anderle) —a post-apocalyptic paranormal adventure

Gateway to the Universe (co-written with Justin Sloan & Michael Anderle)—this book transitions the characters from the Terry Henry Walton Chronicles to The Bad Company

The Bad Company (co-written with Michael Anderle)—a military science fiction space opera

End Times Alaska (also available in audio)—a Permuted Press publication—a post-apocalyptic survivalist adventure

The Free Trader—a Young Adult Science Fiction Action Adventure

Cygnus Space Opera (also available in audio)—A Young Adult Space Opera (set in the Free Trader universe)

Darklanding (co-written with Scott Moon) (also available in audio)— a Space Western

Judge, Jury, & Executioner (also available in audio)—a space opera adventure legal thriller

Rick Banik (also available in audio)—Spy & Terrorism Action Adventure

Successful Indie Author—a non-fiction series to help self-published authors

Metamorphosis Alpha—stories from the world's first science fiction RPG

The Expanding Universe—science fiction anthologies

Shadow Vanguard—a Tom Dublin series

Superdreadnought (co-written with Tim Marquitz)– an AI military space opera

Metal Legion (co-written with Caleb Wachter) (coming in audio)—a military space opera

End Days (co-written with E.E. Isherwood) (coming in audio)—a post-apocalyptic adventure

Mystically Engineered (co-written with Valerie Emerson)—Mystics, dragons, & spaceships

Monster Case Files (co-written with Kathryn Hearst)—A Warner Twins Mystery Adventure

Published exclusively by Craig Martelle, Inc

The Dragon's Call by Angelique Anderson & Craig A. Price, Jr.—an epic fantasy quest

Made in the USA
Las Vegas, NV
06 August 2021